creative ESSENTIALS

Also by Yvonne Grace

Writing for Television: Series, Serials and Soaps

YVONNE GRACE

FROM CREATION TO PITCH
HOW TO WRITE STORIES
FOR TELEVISION THAT SELL

creative ESSENTIALS

First published in 2023 by Creative Essentials,
an imprint of Oldcastle Books
Harpenden, Herts, UK

oldcastlebooks.com
@OldcastleBooks

Series Editor: Hannah Patterson

A CIP catalogue record for this book is available from the British Library.

978-0-85730-533-6 (Paperback)
978-0-85730-534-3 (eBook)

2 4 6 8 10 9 7 5 3 1

Typeset in 10pt on 14pt ITC Franklin Gothic Standard
by Avocet Typeset, Bideford, Devon, EX39 2BP
Printed and bound in Great Britain by
CPI Group (UK) Ltd, Croydon CR0 4YY

MIX
Paper | Supporting
responsible forestry
FSC® C171272
FSC
www.fsc.org

'We are the story of our lives – now let's write'

Yvonne Grace, Script Advice

To all the writers: for turning up to the blank page every day, for digging deep when the inspiration was weak, for putting the work in and for sharing your worlds with me, thank you.

CONTENTS

INTRODUCTION

Three pigeons line up on the fence; you are looking out of the window and begin to imagine that number one and two are Mr and Mrs, and number three is their attractive new neighbour. And now, looking more closely, you can definitely see a glint in Mrs Pigeon's birdy eye. There are two reasons here to identify you as a writer. First, instead of three rather bland, suburban birds, you imagined the beginnings of a tawdry feathered affair. Second, in order to see this drama unfolding in the first place, you were staring out of the window which, as many writers agree, is the same thing as working.

Writing is a creative activity and when you're first embarking on a new concept for a television series, it's guaranteed that you'll be doing a fair amount of metaphorical paint-splashing; throwing all your thoughts and feelings and ideas at the canvas to see what sticks. I love working with writers. I enjoy helping them to explore their creative ideas: rootling around in the narrative rubble, identifying the treasure and discarding the trash, then showing them how to present this gorgeous thing we've discovered in the most constructive way, using the language that producers will understand.

But there are moments during this creative process when I've been known to break out in a rash of anxiety, particularly when writers say things like: 'I don't plan. I just let my mind wander until I find what feels like a start point', or 'I never know where I'm going to end up when I start writing a story, I let my characters decide that', or 'I think outlining hinders my creative process'. Because here's the rub: if you are going to be a successful TV writer, pretty soon you'll be required to address the structure and building blocks of your television world. And if you don't like structuring your stories, you will find writing for television hard. It's hard anyway – doing anything worthwhile takes effort – but it's a tough thing to do well, and giving in to the unbending rule that 'Outlining Is Your Friend' will save you a lot of time, pain and stress from the start.

In preparation for this book, I talked to a carefully picked selection of my favourite television writers, alongside a handful of key producers. Almost all of them will tell you that outlining and structuring is a process that they, to a greater or lesser extent, follow. And what any television producer worth their salt will also tell you is that only a well-structured series will land both creatively and commercially with its audience. Which means that, as television writers, you need to have one foot firmly rooted in creative turf and the other in commercial ground.

In order to help you write with confidence in both these camps, I will explore the different demands of each. I will take you through the process of writing the documents required to pitch, looking at loglines, synopses and treatments; how to storyline and structure your series stories in the best way possible; and how to approach the all-important pilot and make your project shine. The interviews with television colleagues towards the end of the book will also give you a wide variety of professional perspectives on the entire process.

So strap yourself in and come with me as we move from creation to pitch.

THE DEVELOPMENT **JOURNEY**

Before anyone else gets involved, your project will start with just you, and perhaps a white board, or a wall full of sticky notes, or maybe a spreadsheet or a pile of notebooks. Or it may be the cursor on your laptop, blinking... Whatever way you begin this process, you will primarily be having a one-sided conversation with yourself. Yet television is fundamentally collaborative and what I wish for you is to find a like-minded professional with whom you can work to help bring your projects to the fore. That way you are not stuck for too long in your room alone, wrestling with your many-tentacled series idea.

If you are going to be successful at getting your stories out of your head, and out of your room into the wider world, you will need to begin a conversation with a bunch of people who may actually be able to get this thing made. Drama development for television is based on a crucial, sometimes fragile, foundation which is the relationship between the script editor/development exec and the writer.

Drama veteran executive producer Hilary Salmon at the BBC back in the early 1990s said something to me – a wet-behind-the-ears script editor in the series department – that has stayed with me ever since. To be a strong support for writers in this industry we need to be fascinated by them not only as people but as practitioners. We need to be hungry to find out how writers write like they do and why they do it.

As soon as you involve a script editor or development exec in the development of your television project, it will undergo an examination that takes in not only the internal shape of the story but also an entire series overview; and increasingly producers and commissioners are looking to glean suggestions as to how a series 2 may pick up from series 1.

THE ENGAGEMENT, THE CORE, THE CONNECTION, THE LANDING

There are four important elements to a television series that will hit both the commercial and the creative notes, and ultimately land with a receptive, engaged audience. The key here is to create an investment that will pay off in terms of both ratings and tweets on social media. Producers and the platforms that broadcast their product are looking for that holy grail of audience loyalty coupled with commercial recoup of their very expensive outlay. If a series hits the four elements outlined here, it will be a successful show in both critical and commercial circles.

The Engagement Factor is that 'thing' in a story that pulls the reader/viewer in, and it can come from many sources.

Character is most important here. But not just character, it has to be character plus subtext. In *Hacks*, the award-winning HBO/Amazon Prime comedy (penned by a tight writer team and created by Paul W Downs, Jen Statsky and Lucia Aniello), Deborah Vance, the driven, career-focused Las Vegas comic (played by Jean Smart in the performance of her life) would not be nearly so attractive to us if we didn't know what truly drove her to be so ruthless in her personal and professional lives. Her subtext, which the writing beautifully expresses, is all about her abject fear of getting too old to be relevant, of being overlooked and forgotten. The audience know too how hard she has had to fight for her place, albeit now shaky, on the clifftop of success.

A relevant story – and even a period piece must on some level be relevant to its contemporary audience – is another way to create engagement. Consider the hugely successful Netflix period romp *Bridgerton*, created by Chris Van Dusen and executive produced by that very commercially minded showrunner Shonda Rhimes (*Grey's Anatomy/Inventing Anna*). This is a daring, hugely confident and original take on the period genre. Here we have skyscraper wigs and lavish costumes – something we may well expect in a high-end drama series – but there is a unique, and very appealing, theatrical edge. Queen Charlotte's gown and wig-game in particular, steals every scene she's in. Also ensuring a high engagement factor is the style and energy applied to the language, which could be described as 'Colloquial-Baroque'. In short, these people are our people, but in period costume.

The Core of the series is where its commercial aspect truly lies. Here, producers will have identified what makes it tick and made sure that it's easily identifiable; confident that there is both an audience for this particular story and a marketable angle to the series as a whole. We will look more at how that works during the development process in Chapter 2, but some recent examples of strong television series with an identifiable core, which is both creative and commercial, are:

Bad Sisters (Sharon Horgan/Merman Productions/Apple TV). The ensemble of the tight-knit familial group of these engaging, funny, flawed Irish sisters is a massively attractive structural hook and also a means to drive the storyline in a dynamic way, by virtue of the fact that these girls are united in one thing. They all hate John Paul, but they are not all on the same page as to what to do about him.

Slow Horses (Mick Herron/See-Saw Films/Sony/Apple TV). Again, this is an ensemble piece, which is an effective way of structuring a series to ensure maximum engagement, but it is expertly driven through the central character of Lamb, the shambolic old-school agent who knows all the tricks and stopped giving a toss a long time ago. His character is essentially what holds this piece together and makes it a cut above other thriller/espionage formats.

The White Lotus (Mike White/HBO). A line of dialogue delivered by the beleaguered, fractured heiress Tanya McQuoid-Hunt, played by Jennifer Coolidge (who won Best Supporting Actress at the Emmys) – 'These gays, they're trying to murder me' – started trending big-time on Twitter after it streamed. It perfectly encapsulated the creatively brave, dark, twisty nature of this successful anthology series based around a luxury hotel franchise.

Killing Eve (Phoebe Waller-Bridge/Emerald Fennell/Laura Neal/BBC). Villanelle and her nemesis, Eve Polastri, form the darkly disturbing but blackly comic duo at the centre of this cat-and-mouse scenario, and the commercial angles are many. There's murder done stylishly, dialogue that is both acerbic and funny, fabulous locations and clothes, and at the heart of it all, a love story.

The Connection to a series happens in the first instance via the all-important pilot script which must create a positive reaction in the potential producer to go any further. This can be on a commercial level but also, more often than not, it is on an emotional level. There is a reason why writers like Russell T Davies, Sally Wainwright and Jed Mercurio write such successful television series. They understand the importance of connection in storytelling. Their processes no doubt differ, but I am sure that early on in their series' development they addressed the over arc of the series they wanted to write and found ways of making connections between the central characters and their storylines.

This is the territory I came into, very green and eager to learn, at Granada in 1993. I was hot off the back of a year script editing *EastEnders* which was riding high in the ratings war at the time and giving *Coronation Street* a run for its money. Very quickly, in a room with the likes of Russell T and Sally W, I got used to discussing story with a confidence that I didn't at the time feel. But during this intense period, I realise now, looking back, that I was in a crucible of creativity where story was everything and it always came from character. Our discussions were not so much about the five-act structure of television storytelling that I teach today, nor about the jump off, midpoint and landing format which I now use to help my writers shape their storylines. There was no formula and no official structural analysis going on. But we all, to a person, understood innately how to make a storyline tick. What process was needed to get it truly going and what would be the 'thing' that got an audience hooked to the end. This was a lot to do with understanding the story engine – literally what was driving the story through the series arc as a whole.

Over a period of five intense years I worked with Russell, Sally, Paul Abbott, Kay Mellor, and many other writers who are still doing their amazing thing to this day. It was here that I learned how to handle long-running series narrative. And the key to all of it is how to make a dramatic, emotional connection with the characters in the fictional world you are creating, and with your viewers in the real world, outside the small screen.

A producer is looking, possibly without even realising it, for elements in a script that will form the bedrock of a creative, commercial series: the hooks, cliffs and set pieces. The business of story development and structure is often aided very well by the use of imagery, and the hook – used a great deal in soap structure – immediately gives the writer the image necessary to understand what it is that the script needs to do at this point. Whether this is a specific visual, a revelatory line of dialogue or a sequence of events, the job here is to literally hook the viewer into the next episode.

'Cliff' is another soap term but can be applied to all good series storytelling. What is it that you're ending on and why would your audience return? Set pieces are a combination of the subtext, the text and a strong visual that wraps around the two key storytelling elements to create a perfect representation of the series you are watching as a whole. An example of a set piece in drama might be the scene in *Bad Sisters,* when the Garvey siblings are all gathered in eldest sister Eva's garden. On a spike is a melon, which represents the hateful head of John Paul – their nemesis. Each one takes their turn in trying to hit a bullseye with their ineffectual bow and arrow skills. Bibi (not hindered by her eyepatch) is nearest to hitting the target. Will this be enough to kill him?

The Landing – the way the series ends should, in my opinion, be considered at the point of conception. A strong, commercial and creative series – no matter how many series or seasons there are of the show – will have a feeling of cohesion throughout its time span. This will be achieved by attention not only to the overall tone of the show, but more crucially to how the storylines, spanning across this timeline, weave and connect. Storylining is key to a coherent, truly immersive series, and its flow needs to be controlled from the outset. We need an engaging beginning, a middle where the storylines are expanded and explored, and a defined, impactful landing.

Series 1 and 2 of *Happy Valley* (BBC1) are so interconnected that I am sure Sally Wainwright would have had a strong idea about where she was going to take the main characters of Catherine Cawood and her bête noire

Tommy Lee Royce in series 2, when first conceiving of series 1. And the final series 3 is a tour de force in how to tie up all the story strands from across the arc of all three series. Sally understands the way to create narrative stretch and connection throughout the arc of the series. She creates not obvious, but realistic, crossover points for all her main characters and by drilling constantly into the subtext of what is driving them, we have what appears to be a free-flowing, uninterrupted and natural progression of storyline for each major player. This looks effortless but it takes a seasoned expert at handling series narrative like this to make it appear easy. The structure is all there – but we, the audience, do not see the joins.

MY DEVELOPMENT PROCESS:
CREATIVE VS COMMERCIAL

Setting up my script consultancy in 2013, I realised that in order to truly help writers develop and produce really great stories and scripts for television, I had to not only analyse, but also write down the process I use with the writers I work with. There is a school of thought that says the creative process is 90 per cent instinctive and only 10 per cent prescriptive. I don't agree with this. To my mind, the creative process is a 50/50 split between the ideas and the application. The creative free flow and the prescriptive work. I realised there had to be a formula somewhere in all of this that I could pass on to my writers so they could use it going forward, to create solid television series narratives, when I wasn't in the room or breathing down their necks via Zoom.

As we've established, my big ethos, and the one I carry with me always when working with writers, is this: ***all series television stories need to be both creatively engaging and commercially successful.*** I put on my producer hat when I read your work, or discuss with you the world you want to create. Producers do not like to have to dig through reams of extraneous stuff to get to the core of the story you are writing. They want to be hand-fed. They want everything to be clear, engaging and to say something about our world today.

The zeitgeist is at play here. Producers want to feel the work they develop and produce is both relevant and in whatever way you fashion it, will somehow hit the zeitgeist. They love a television angle. It's all about the way you package and present your television series which will ensure they have to say yes, when they are always actively looking for a reason to say no. So, not only is it vital your story is creatively strong, it has to be commercially viable, and this comes down to the prescriptive elements I mentioned in the previous chapter. You need a particular mindset to ensure you are writing commercially as well as creatively, and here I will try and impart my specific development process, which I hope will bring you clarity when you are knee-deep in a new idea and inspire you to carry on.

WHAT'S THE BIG PICTURE?
MACRO VS MICRO VIEWPOINTS

The biggest mistake writers make when they come to me with a new series they want to develop is they have invariably focused on the detail, not the big picture. So my first question, and the one that often is the hardest one to answer, is, 'What's the big picture?' What I mean by this question is, 'What is the overall message of your story?' Or put another way, 'What is it that you really want to say?'

This is the macro viewpoint of the series as a whole. I will refer often to the macro viewpoint. To my mind this is both the bigger picture of the story you are telling incrementally across a series arc of time, and it also represents the audience's viewpoint as they observe your story unfolding on screen. The macro viewpoint is tied into the actual fabric of the series structure. For example, in a procedural drama like *Casualty* or *Line of Duty*, the macro viewpoint is the hospital and its staff and the members of the AC12 unit and their police world respectively. In the Netflix series *Criminal*, created by Jim Field Smith and George Kay, it is the psychologically tricky world of interrogation and in *Detectorists* (BBC/Netflix, written by Mackenzie Crook), the macro view is the far gentler world of metal detecting.

Identify at the outset what your macro viewpoint is and then we can consider the micro viewpoint. This is the point of view of those characters living in the world you create. They are seeing their world from the inside out and we, the macro viewers, are seeing it from the outside in. For example, Catherine Cawood in *Happy Valley* (written by Sally Wainwright BBC/Red Productions series 1 and 2 and Lookout Point Productions series 3), takes the micro viewpoint, and ultimately we see everything through her eyes. The micro view in *The Marvelous Mrs Maisel*, created by Amy Sherman-Palladino and Dan Palladino for Amazon Prime Video, is Mrs Maisel – Midge. And in the drama series *Gangs of London*, written by Gareth Evans and Matt Flannery (Sky Atlantic/Pulse and Sister Productions), the micro viewpoint is with a powerful ensemble.

THE BICYCLE WHEEL

This is where my tried and tested visual comes into play – the bicycle wheel. This is a useful visual aid to the essential shape of all good series narratives. The wheel represents both the series as a whole and each individual episode. At the centre of the bicycle wheel sits the smaller wheel. This is where your characters are. But not all of your characters. Crucially, this is where your central characters, those who carry the most narrative weight, sit.

Sometimes, as in, for example, Sharon Horgan's *Bad Sisters*, the centre of the wheel is populated by an ensemble of characters – all carrying similar narrative weight. Although in the case of *Bad Sisters*, I would suggest Eva Garvey, played by Sharon Horgan, takes on a heavier narrative weight, certainly in the earlier episodes of the series. This changes as the series develops and this is structurally a good thing.

Writers often mistakenly imagine structure to be a solid immovable element in their screenwriting toolbox. But it is not. It can be a flexible, supple thing that, whilst framing the series as a whole, can be used to further highlight the ongoing development of a character or characters in your series. Structure is your friend when it comes to presenting creative narratives for television.

The central focus – the smaller wheel in the big wheel of the episode – can shift as the story unfolds. This happens in the *Breaking Bad* spinoff, the award-winning *Better Call Saul*, created by Vince Gilligan and produced by Gilligan/ Bob Odenkirk, who also stars in the lead role, for Netflix/ AMC. Initially the world is all about Jimmy McGill and his metamorphosis into Saul Goodman – but as the seasons developed, so too did his partner in crime, resulting in Kim Wexler becoming as narrative-heavy as Saul in the final season of this brilliant show.

The other characters – those that explore and reveal the procedural element in, for example, *Happy Valley* – are crucial in shaping and linking the police work and its storylines into and around the central storyline of Catherine herself, her back story and her driving subtext. Those characters form a bigger wheel around the central wheel where Catherine sits. All storylines come out from the centre, bisecting and cutting across those generated by the characters in the bigger wheel. The story information goes back and forth between these wheels and so out to inform and engage us, the macro view, watching from our sofas.

It is the flipping between the macro and the micro viewpoints that keeps the story engine of the series pushing forward, ensuring we, the audience, are engaged. I work with the macro vs micro viewpoint to begin to shape the world you want to present before we begin the breaking down of this overview.

THE NARRATIVE THROUGHLINE – THE NECKLACE

The other visual I use a lot in my work with writers is the necklace. This is a way of showing in a simplistic form, the basic structure of a television series story which ensures that all elements in the world you are creating link and connect. Because this is what we are essentially doing when we tell stories in a series format. We are setting up a premise, then breaking it down incrementally across a period of time and via a certain number of episodes; and this step-by-step way of telling stories needs a clear, connective framework.

Once you have got that framework in place, then you will always take your audience with you along this often layered, complex path. The framework here is the necklace. Each episode must connect and link to the overall narrative throughline, like beads hanging on the same string of the necklace. Each bead – or episode – is threaded through its centre to the string, which to my mind represents the narrative throughline of the series as a whole. In this way, theme and message – what you want to say – is clear and engaging to an audience.

To my commercially wired brain, the title of your series is the same thing as the narrative throughline. The title will link, connect and thematically hold together your series. Examples of titles that do all this very well are some of the shows I have already mentioned: *Bad Sisters*, *Happy Valley*, *Better Call Saul*. Other favourites include *Godless* (Netflix), whose title thematically links to a strong metaphor running throughout the show, *Sex Education* (Netflix), which does what is says on the tin whilst also adding an ironic note, and *Halt and Catch Fire* (AMC) which is the command the earliest computers would issue if they were about to malfunction. Thematically, tonally and structurally these titles present something of the story that's about to unfold, and deliver a punch that makes an audience want to check out the series. That is why, very early on in the creative process, I encourage my writers to come up with a title that both speaks to them and taps into the bigger picture of their series story. If you do this early on in the development process, you will find your creative decisions are also dictated by the impact of your title.

SHAPE THE STORY VISUALLY

I have been in the business of development and production for 30 years, and I have a way of working with writers that has never let me down. However, it was only when I was setting up Script Advice that I realised something fundamental that I needed to impart to the creatives I intended to work with. *I don't read words when reading a script, I read pictures.* It is my view that producers worth their salt also primarily work visually. Television is a visual medium after all.

At the creative beginning of a project with a writer, these are the questions I have in my mind which need answering. And all the way along the development path, they will keep on coming up, to be addressed and readdressed. If they are not addressed early on, and you do manage to get through the door of a potential producer, these are the questions they will ask anyway, so it serves you well to sort the essentials out from the get go.

Story Impact: Does this story tell me something? Does the world grip me? Do I want to keep turning the page?

Character Development: Are these people credible, relevant and engaging? Do I care about any of them?

Visualisation: Does the story translate visually? Can I see this unfolding on the screen?

Audience Connection: Can I put myself in this story? Can I connect with these people and this world in a social, moral, psychological or emotional way?

Increasingly, I find novelists want to work with me to adapt their novels to the television series format. This is a very good thing to my mind, as often, speaking from a producer's point of view, using the intellectual and creative property of a novel to form a strong series format gives a commissioner a sense of security at the outset. The novel, if it has already found an audience, is a far less daunting prospect than a series that has not found its niche.

The problem with adapting a novel to television is that the story which is described using words on the page in a novel may not translate well to the screen if the writer cannot use pictures, in a large part, to replace all those words. I mention novels as creative source material because they are a solid seam to plunder, but be aware that television and novels are entirely different creatures, and their story language is as different as English and Greek.

You need a strong ear for dialogue, a robust understanding of character, but most importantly you need a visual imagination to tell television stories well. Working with writers visually is the key to getting a commercial and creative project ready for the market. Always refer back to that old adage 'show don't tell'. Using your visual imagination – your mind's eye – build the story for your character/s across your series timeline in an incremental sequence of visual scenes.

Identify what it is you want your audience to know and feel in this moment and then shape your scene around this intention. Use visuals to bring out the emotion or the message in a scene or sequence of scenes. For example, so many times we have seen two people in a domestic situation – one in love, the other not. Often the first impulse for a writer evoking the break-up scene for an audience is to fall back on explanation, talking all the feelings out. Character A's POV, then character B's. Instead, consider first the subtext and then add the dialogue when the picture has done enough. Perhaps character A is doing all the talking (her subtext is that she is doing so to hide the fact that she cheated and feels bad about it). Character B does not say a word. But the pencil he happens to be holding snaps in two and we end that moment on her face as she realises that he knows and that she's going to have to face up to it.

Producers and commissioners are a skittish lot. There's so much at stake when taking on a new drama series. Not only the amount of money involved in making them, which is increasingly eyewateringly expensive, but also the various layers of people that need to be satisfied. The process of commissioning and producing is a risk-averse business – as I said earlier in this chapter – so make sure you don't give those that hold the money and access a chance to say no.

THE CREATIVE AND COMMERCIAL
MINDSET

Inspiration comes from many places and no one writer's process is the same as another's. However, there are some fundamental elements that, once inspiration has struck, you need to make sure are in your creative thinking as you go forward. It is not uncommon for a writer to be all fired up about an idea they want to explore with me, only to discover, when they dig into the narrative and explore their characters, that it comes apart like tissue paper in their hands. This is usually because the idea they have is just that – a series of visually alluring, potentially exciting moments. An idea without a centre or a strong throughline. Stories have progression built into their DNA. Ideas or moments may, if put together in the right way, show some promise as the beginning of a story arc, but momentum needs to be built into the concept in order for the building blocks you are trying to construct to become a supporting wall.

THE POWER OF THE ARC

I will go into more detail about arcs and how I use them in my development work, and how they can help you structure your work for maximum impact, in Chapter 9. But I want to discuss them in this chapter too, because they are a vital part of the creative and commercial mindset for a writer. The series arc ensures there's a strong trajectory for the story which is, essentially, mapped out along the series timeline via the individual character arcs.

Character creates plot. Never the other way around. A character is driven by the internal subtext: that which makes them go out into the world and start making things happen, in a physical echo of their internal, emotional desire. Through intention, so plot is created. If you get used to thinking in terms of arcs for your characters – what their main trajectory is across the potential timeline of the series – you will be able to see, in the initial stages, if your story does in fact have 'legs' or if it is actually another bundle of great moments, which have no progression or connection to the over arcing theme you wish to explore.

Arcs also suggest, like the separate colour stripes in a rainbow, a transition from A to B with an incline that reaches a zenith point, travels along a bit, then comes down the other side to land. This is the thinking you need to adopt in order to shape your story arcs for your characters at the start of your creative process. Fashioning a rough arc for everyone is key to the world you envision, and creates a mindset that a commercially successful television story needs.

Producers look for story drive – the energy of the narrative – its purpose. Here there needs to be progression, build

THE CREATIVE AND COMMERCIAL MINDSET

and landing. They may not use these words per se in your development conversations, or they may not be aware that this is what they are looking for, but said out loud or not, this is what they want.

This is the language I was surrounded by when first starting out as a development script editor in the drama series department of the BBC and then Granada Television. Here I worked with many writers who are now at the very height of their powers – Sally Wainwright and Russell T Davies, as previously mentioned, but also, during my BBC days, high-calibre writers such as Tony Jordan (CEO of the hugely successful production company Red Planet that makes, amongst many hit shows, *Death in Paradise*), Ashley Pharoah (co-creator and writer of the massive commercial hit *Life on Mars*) and Matthew Graham (*Life on Mars* and *Electric Dreams*).

Working up an idea from scratch with a writer during this fertile period of the mid to late 1990s, the first conversation we would have would be all about identifying the over arcing series narrative. Then it would be about each individual character arc. Then we would start shaping the episodes into broad-stroke series arcs. And finally, we'd break down the pilot episode, once we felt the general arc of the series was in place. The questions in the back of our minds here were always, 'What's the angle into the story?' and 'How do we present this – what does the package look like?' These were the days of *Cracker* and of *Prime Suspect,* and we were influenced by the way these commercially strong, character-driven pieces had immediate traction and engagement from their audiences.

Today, the modern world of television development and production is defined by the need for brilliant stories to be told episodically across long-format lengths so streamers have the content they need and we can binge to our heart's content. There's a skill to creating that episodic weight, which I hope this book will go some way to explaining.

Thinking of examples of more recent, strongly presented and packaged series, *Sex Education* (Laurie Nunn/Netflix) and *Vigil* (Tom Edge/World Productions) come to mind. *Sex Education* is packaged very cleverly visually. It does not look like a typical UK series and has the tone and visual punch of a US youth/school-centric series. An ensemble piece, each character in it has a very muscular, layered storyline and the young characters drive the story whilst the adult characters are woven around their dynamic – the youth of the series informing and altering the adults. In *Vigil*, it is a claustrophobic thriller plot driven by strong forceful characters, focused essentially on the micro viewpoint of DCI Silva, played by Suranne Jones. The submarine is a character here, and it's because of where she is and why she is there that this particular thriller pans out the way it does.

The most important conversations we had then (and I still have with my writers now) are about the key moments, and the visuals and story threads that got us to those landmarks. The series arc will change as the project develops but when you have got to a broad-stroke trajectory you are happy with, it's time to consider what the pilot will look like.

BEGIN WITH A VISUAL

This visual needs to set the scene. This is the moment you are beginning your story and the journey of your characters starts here. You are also setting up the series arc in these crucial first moments. Often a geographical view or some sort of pertinent visual, particular to the environment that forms the backdrop of your series, is a good way in. *Nolly*, by Russell T Davies for ITVX/Quay Street Productions, gives us a strong visual that takes us back to the first colour recording, and frames for us not only the world of television production as it was then, but also the start of the career of the young star of this perfectly formed three-parter, Noele Gordon.

BEGIN THE NARRATIVE

Do you want to impart a raw emotion, or a plot point, or both? This is all about connecting immediately to your audience via the first words spoken. Don't waste them. Start a series of sparks that the audience will remember later in the episode. *Bloodline*, by Todd and Glenn Kessler and Daniel Zelman for Netflix, begins very atmospherically with a voiceover by the 'good' brother as the 'bad' brother sleeps on the Greyhound bus which we watch curve along the coast road of the bay, ocean and landscape that the series will be set against.

BRING IN THE AURAL

Sound can be just as emotive a tool as the visuals in storytelling, and creative writers should be using both, not only to work together, but also as counterpoints to one another. Overlapping the sound to the image we are seeing, or starting with black, with the sound as the only thing that's assaulting our senses, are decisions you need to make in the first few seconds of the pilot. You are creating a tone, a stamp of style and intent here using sound as well as the visual. In *Nine Perfect Strangers*, for example, the adaptation of the Liane Moriarty novel for Hulu, we hear the buzz of a food blender then see the healthy contents being pulverised, which is overlaid with the sounds of nature as the day dawns in this exclusive health spa.

PLAY WITH LANGUAGE

How the dialogue is used in these first crucial moments can deepen the emotional experience for the viewer but also impart a sense of the subtext driving beneath the character. Dialogue sets the tone, style and period of the story. Use this symbiotically with the visuals – both need equal weight here. Play with the language in your story. How a character expresses themselves is just as revealing as what they look like and what they do.

HOW DOES THIS CUT?

When I read a script with my producer hat on, I do two things simultaneously. I read the words on the page but I see the scene visually. This is a double-edged attack on the sensibilities of firstly your reader, and ultimately your audience. Get used to 'cutting' the scenes together in your head – your mind's eye – as you write them. There's a natural rhythm here that you will begin to feel as you go through the pilot. You will be aware of what has gone before and what you are travelling towards. Television writers need to be asking themselves, 'What happened before, now what happens next?' all the time. This question should be hitting you in the back of the neck as you write – never rest up and let the narrative pace dawdle.

DOES EACH SCENE EARN ITS PLACE?

The job of a scene is essentially two-fold:

1. To explain the plot – visually and using dialogue – therefore pushing the narrative forward.
2. To explore the subtext – to dig into what motivates your characters.

If both the subtext and the text are working together, then your narrative will feel buoyant and your reader/audience will be engaged. You can withhold information that the micro view doesn't know – i.e. those in the world

– which the macro view (the audience) does, or flip that process. You can highlight a piece of action or information, you can mystify and intrigue but you must make sure your scene does something. Travelling scenes that do not push story, or holding scenes that repeat or stagnate the story, are not doing their job. Once you've got the first draft done – the vomit draft – these are the types of scenes you will be cutting out.

TOWARDS A **STRONGER STORY**

The creative process is, as any writer will tell you, a personal, specific and unique activity. So I am not going to go into a great diatribe about how important it is to put your behind down on the seat each day and produce x amount of pages. I assume, unless you follow Hemingway and write standing up, that you do sit down to do the deed and the amount of pages you produce is entirely up to you – to some writers a page a day is a great achievement, to others it represents slacking. I would suggest you form a habit, however long you work at your pages, of doing so every day at the time of day that you feel most works for you. I work with writers who start as early as 5am and do a couple of hours before their day properly starts. Others don't sit down to work until late morning, after the school run, having loaded the dishwasher, or taken the dog for a walk. Others work really late at night when everyone else is asleep. Horses for courses. It's all creative endeavour which must be applauded so I will leave the specifics for you to organise and channel as you see fit.

But I do want to metaphorically pop my head around your door to give you three main steps to making sure the stories you are creating for television tick specific boxes, and all this effort you are putting in pays dividends in the long run. If you follow these steps your story has a good chance of developing from tiny, weightless embryo, to staggering, struggling toddler and finally full-grown hairy teenager who's demanding food whilst welded to the Xbox.

PINPOINT THE CENTRAL THRUST OF THE NARRATIVE: In every story there's a message that runs through it. It can be a straight and linear path, like the word Blackpool through a stick of rock, but it can also ripple throughout the narrative like raspberry sauce through ice-cream. However you choose to distribute your message structurally in your script, make sure there is one and that you know what it is.

IDENTIFY WHO OR WHAT DRIVES THE STORY FROM SCENE TO SCENE: In every story there is a character central to the plot and the message – he/she sits at the centre of your story, and therefore your script, like that circle in the middle of a bicycle wheel from where all storylines (and bike spokes) radiate. It may be that you have an ensemble – a group of characters who fulfil this function – but you need to make sure you know who they are and why they are in this pivotal position both structurally and in terms of narrative.

WHAT MOTIVATES YOUR CHARACTER/S? In every story there is a strong and powerful subtext chugging away underneath the action and this is what you need to make sure is working in every scene – as an underpin and a counterpoint to the action and the words on the page.

It helps from the outset to give yourself clear bullet points from which to work as you begin to expand and deliver your television series project.

MAPPING AND STRUCTURE: THE MACRO VS THE MICRO VIEW: It's best to keep structural questions as simple as possible. So ask yourself, 'What do I really want to say?' Then use the macro vs micro ideas explored in Chapter 2 to frame your world from the outset. Start getting the bones of the story done, by identifying what is the macro viewpoint (the backdrop or bigger picture) and what is the micro viewpoint (whose point of view are we following?)

CHARACTER ARCS: Controlling the arc of both your series as a whole and that of your characters individually will ensure your series has impact. So you need to identify here what the main points are along that particular storyline for each character. This applies to any character who holds narrative weight in your series. Take your character in big giant steps across the span of their story arc, from episode 1 to the end point. There is no need at this point to map out every beat, but do identify the jump off, the midpoint and the landing for everyone. As you continue to develop your series outline, you will be able to fill in further detail as you drill into the subtext of your characters.

WRITING THE TREATMENT AND IDENTIFYING THE DNA OF YOUR TV SERIES: In Chapter 11, I present my treatment template. This is a simple, clear way of laying out the various elements needed to both present and explore the character arcs, the series outline, the episodes and the pilot which will hopefully sell the rest of the series.

OUTLINING THE SERIES: Nailing the narrative throughline. Again, use broad strokes to begin with. The first few episodes in your series will seed and set up the arc for all the key players. The middle episodes are doing the exploring and expanding part of the series arc. The end episodes are paying off the initial seeding and tying up the various strands so you can land the story effectively in the last episode. Think rule of three: Seed. Explore. Payoff.

THE FIRST 10 PAGES OF YOUR PILOT OR HOW THE FIRST 10 PAGES SELL THE OTHER 50: In a five-act structure, Act 1 will set up and seed all the jump off points for the key characters sitting at the centre of the wheel of the episode (and the series as a whole). Page 10 is the 10th minute in a TV hour – make sure all the storylines have been started for all key players by this point to ensure your audience is hooked in and engaged. Main points for the first 10 pages of your pilot to address are:

Draw In: Use a strong visual or an impactful sequence via dialogue and action.

Engage: Character dynamic, information regarding plot, emotionally driven from the subtext.

Hold: A strong visual, or a sequence that ties in both subtext and text, working with a dynamic action or section of dialogue between the key players. Hold the audience's attention.

Challenge: Something unusual or intriguing is now going on in the plot line to challenge the audience.

Push On: Keep the plot moving. Do not meander or stagnate. Now you are through the first 10 minutes and into Act 2, your audience should still be with you.

THE FIRST DRAFT OF THE PILOT – THE VOMIT DRAFT

Get through the five acts with a forward driving energy and visual mindset. Make sure at least one peak occurs in each act in the storyline. So we have a sense of creating a series of peaks of varying lengths throughout the pilot. Get these in place and then you can go back to rewrite and reshape and hone the full thing. Identify in the Vomit Draft the jump off, mid- and land points in the arc of the episode as a whole.

FOUR DOCUMENTS THAT
START AND CONTINUE
THE PRODUCER CONVERSATION

To write television drama well, to converse with those who can make your drama a reality, to sell yourself as a creative talent and your ideas as viable, you need to have a dual mindset. There is art, of course, to what we do, but in my opinion writers in television are a specific breed: they are the artists who need to understand how and what sells their work. Essentially, there are three things to keep in mind when you embark on any creative endeavour aimed at the television makers and audience.

WRITE FROM THE HEART: MEAN WHAT YOU SAY AND SAY WHAT YOU MEAN

Choose your words carefully. Do not meander, or shilly-shally. Aim for what it is you truly mean and say that. And only that. Every time. Stay true to the original idea – the essence of what you want to say – and your discussions will always come from a place of integrity. You will gain confidence this way.

ASSUME NOTHING

Do not make the mistake of believing that the producer reading this treatment/outline/pilot will understand what you know to be true in your story. You need to make sure the text and what lies beneath it – the subtext – are both as clear as each other. Do not assume the person/people with whom you are attempting to communicate automatically speak your particular lingo. Make every creative choice regarding plotline, tone, character development and visuals in a decisive, committed manner. The clarity of what you are saying and how you are saying it will make all assumptions null and void. There will be no need to assume because your communication is creatively clear.

DON'T TAKE CRITICISM PERSONALLY

Writing television drama, or indeed any creative endeavour, is entirely subjective. Great writers such as Tony Jordan, Shonda Rhimes and Aaron Sorkin are also people who put the human experience right at the centre of what they write about. This is the stuff of feeling, of emotion, of need, ambition and desire. As an audience member, when we watch shows like *Hustle* (Tony Jordan), *Grey's Anatomy* (Shonda Rhimes) or *The West Wing* (Aaron Sorkin), we are being invited by the writer to enter a world they shaped from the page outwards. Your experience of this viewing will be two things simultaneously: personal to you and understood by many.

As your project develops, with the input of those people that can make it happen, you will receive many notes, many opinions and many ideas. Take none of them to your own personal heart. This is about the work. It is an extension of you but it is not you. Own what you create and then get used to sharing it, quickly, without issue. Be the writer everyone likes to work with.

This is why I love television. Things happen to deadline. There is very little procrastination or 'messing around'. This is because producers are cash rich but time poor. They want your ideas. They want your talent. They don't like to read much and they make decisions pretty quickly. Time is money. So you need to harness your creative brain and give them your fabulous imagination, story and characters in the format they expect and with a professional, succinct, engaging aplomb.

FOUR DOCUMENTS TELEVISION PRODUCERS LOVE

1. THE PITCH PAGE

A sheet of A4. The whole story – from the beginning, through the middle and to the end – presented succinctly, in an engaging tone and with just the right amount of 'fizz' to the language to entice and hold your potential producer. At the centre, like that little circle in the middle of a bicycle wheel, sits your main character or characters. From this point outwards all your storylines radiate like spokes on that bicycle wheel. Get the essence of your story down. Distil it to its essence. This is the Pitch Page. This is a good way to help you, even before you begin to discuss your story with anyone in the industry, to genuinely hone your idea to its major component parts. The process of writing this will make you identify the flow of the narrative, what the over arcing themes are and what, essentially, you want to say. The pitch page is not necessary in every developmental conversation. Write one anyway, though, because as I have said before, producers want to be steered in a certain direction; they don't want to have to read reams of material and have to come to their own conclusions. They will at the end of the day, but you want to avoid the response, 'I didn't know what I was meant to be feeling about this. It's not clear.' A pitch page will give you (and them) clarity.

2. THE TREATMENT

The Treatment – and my template is in Chapter 11 – is the central document to your developmental conversation with your potential producer. Here you need to lay out in an easy-to-read, easy-to-assimilate format:

- The Title
- The Format
- The Story in Essence
- The Character Story Arcs
- The Episode Outline
- The Broad Strokes of the Storylines

Increasingly, treatments are getting longer in the developmental process but I still suggest no more than 10 pages to my writers. Sometimes, but not always, producers like visual images to further augment the story and the world you are portraying. The key to writing a good treatment is to keep the character central to the discussion, so as to avoid any feeling of 'format' or conversations about whether the piece is derivative or not. The treatment needs to highlight what is special, different and unique to you, the writer, and the world you portray. It's all about how you come at the story – how interesting you make that trajectory and how you shape our first impression of it.

3. THE SERIES OUTLINE

This is the story as it pans out across the series format as a whole. In this age of streamers, the appetite for stories with narrative stretch and formats of more than six episodes is very strong. Map yours out in broad strokes, the main over arcing storylines of each episode, bringing it all together at the end of the series arc. Producers want to be reassured of the longevity – the staying power – of this series idea but they do not need to know, nor will they want to, how every minute pans out. This is a mutually creative conversation framed in a commercial context. When a producer puts their time and therefore their money into a project, they will want their input felt so do not prescriptively write the storyline for every episode in detail. Collaboration is key here.

4. THE EPISODE OUTLINE

A producer will want to know how the first episode pans out. What are the main peaks, or points of critical impact in the first episode and what are the elements that bring us in and keep us there? How does it start, what is the midpoint and how does it end? Whom do we follow and why, and what do they (and the audience) learn?

These documents are the shorthand for a longer and much more layered and complex conversation you will have with your potential producer, your script editor and yourself.

Get used to having to express yourself in clear, succinct, well-structured formats. Producers will love dealing with you and you will grow both creatively and in your commercial prowess if you nail the writing of these key documents.

STUDIES ON **HOW TO WORK CREATIVELY** WITH DIFFERENT KINDS OF WRITERS

Development executive, script consultant, script editor, development producer. These are all titles that can be applied to the job I do and also the person you will come across, hopefully in a positive way, over your creative life as a writer in television. The job, to my mind, is divided into two Venn diagrams. One called 'Experience' and the other 'Psychology'. Where the two cross over – that sweet segment in the middle – is where the best work is done. It's a job of two halves – 50 per cent of it drilling into the experience I have of working with television stories from the ground up and 50 per cent understanding the motivations and the reactions of the writers I work with and then using that to shape the way I conduct the script edit sessions.

This is a creative and psychological process we are engaged in. Half of the creative process is about 'reading' the writer I am working with from the outset, to ensure I hit the ground running with them. There is no time to 'work things out' when a writer comes to me with their project. Sometimes this is because they are under deadlines from their producer or production company to get their treatment or pilot right, and they are keen to get that process started.

Other times it is because I am working with them for a finite period of time to get their project development fully worked out and packaged right for the market.

In the first instance, I tend to talk around the ideas the writer first had about the world they want to create. I talk about character, the backdrop against which the story unfolds, the connections between the characters, their back stories and through this conversation, themes and longer storylines start to appear. There needs to be flexibility on the part of the writer here. If they are too set within the framework they applied before they brought their project to my development table, they will not allow it to be expanded and so improved. So it's a game of reading the room (or Zoom) and acting accordingly – with speed and making it look natural and without effort. This comes with practice. Like anything worth doing, there are pitfalls and there are mistakes made, but overall, the writer is happy with the end product and I am happy they are. Win-win.

There are as many mindsets as there are writers in this industry, but I have noticed over the years of doing this job that there are rough categories that writers and their projects fall into. Perhaps you recognise your type?

JACKSON POLLOCK

This writer thinks in pictures which is great for television development. Producers do that too, so this writer is already talking their language. The emphasis here is not on the written word, but on the shape and look of a sequence of scenes that go a long way to exploring the underlying message and themes of the story. But this writer is also messy. Structure is not their friend. If truth be told, they fear it. I realise this early on in our relationship. Not to worry – this is where a strong script editor can make all the difference to this writer's confidence and ability to finish the project strongly. Working with this writer, we spend more time brainstorming and getting down the overall shape of the series without too much emphasis on the nuts and bolts of how the story works across the series arc. This is a good way to work with a Jackson Pollock-type creative. They need to literally splash paint around, to talk the character out with me. We exchange ideas to generate story (with me careful not to take over the conversation) and then, when there's enough dramatic paint to work with, I allow it to pool in places. Then we draw lines out from this initial splatter in order to start structuring their character arcs and the storyline of each episode in broad strokes. This structural work will feel as though it has happened organically which is exactly how this writer wants to work.

ESCHER

This writer is too interested in the structure and not enough in the character development. Their project will probably already be a fair way along when they come to me. Inevitably, when there is too much emphasis on clever internal structuring, they have come unstuck and now have got a bit lost as to why they are writing the series in the first place. Sometimes the clever aspect of an idea – the conceit of it – can overshadow the heart of the story. 'Style over Content' is another way of putting it. Often the Escher writer has a complicated, high-concept piece they want to explore and have been carrying this thing around in their head and in various documents on their laptop for a while. They are now so immersed in the ideas and the world they have created that it all appears clear and obvious to them. Until an outside eye, in this case me, reads their outlines and their scripts – usually there is more than one script, which is a Big Red Flag to me – and I have to admit to them in our first Zoom that I am confused. What's the overall concept here? What is it you really want to say? Rule of thumb, writers: if you can't sum up in a few lines what the series is actually about then there is a problem inherent in the initial concept. So with an Escher-type writer we go back to basics. I am a Structure Ninja but this writer doesn't need my input on that front right now. Let's go back to why you wanted to write this in the first place. In many ways, the writer who comes to me with the whole thing almost worked out, episode by episode, like the Escher writer does, is a real joy for me. It's like peeling an onion. With some tears. I help them unpeel all the structure they have in place, all those key moments they think they're heading towards, all those tricksy ideas – the non-linear timeline, the flip of reality, the flashbacks, the reverses – and then, and it always happens somewhere along the line, we get to that moment. The moment where they wanted to start in the first place and then I realise what it is they want to say and why. So we build from there. Upwards.

MONDRIAN

Boxes, primary colours, grids. This writer has structure at their heart but in terms of their storylines, they have key 'Big Bold Moments' they want to hit and they are doing it with an emphasis on these without paying attention to the build-up and the subtlety that's necessary. Good television writing is structurally strong, but the audience must never be able to see the joins of that structure. The other common drawback with this type of writer and their project is that they are starting their story too far back in their timeline. So much of what they want to do here, to get to the first big red box in their storyline, is set-up and explanation. Their instinct is to hold off on the truly interesting moments of their story and so fall back on treading water dramatically until they feel the time is right for things to get interesting. Red Flags start unfurling for me... This sort of writer will have a clear idea of the major building blocks of their story across their series. It is also not uncommon for the writer to have mapped out what they see would be the story from series 2 onwards. The worst has happened in this case. This writer, from a place of good intent and hard work, has practically written the whole outline for series 1. As a result, they have nailed down the big plot beats, thus cementing the ways in which the story unfolds, across not only the first series but also the second. Ninety-nine per cent of the time they will not have got the story flow correct across such a big expanse of time. Working individually in this way, confronted as it were by a full series to storyline and deliver, the writer has understandably attacked their story with the focus of a pneumatic drill. However, when creating a complex scenario of interweaving storylines, the key thing to remember is: keep the initial planning broad and general. Beat out the jump off, midpoint and landing of each of the main characters and then go back along your story wall to fill in the detail. A lot of television development is about broadly stretching a dramatic scenario over a long timeline and then going back to condense it again, so you can write a clear, succinct series outline and a treatment that will sell the project but that comes in at the ten-page mark. More on that in another chapter.

THE ONE SCENE

The hardest form of development for a script editor but, in many ways, the most rewarding. The writer has come to me with literally one idea and wants to make this the core of a series for television. The idea is often contained in one scene effectively. So we start from the ground up. I do a lot of work here on character development. All character is plot. Plot comes from character. It is never applied from the top down. The plot comes from underneath the action/text and from a point of emotional engagement within the character. This is literally their subtext, in that the plot is driving forward from an internal submerged place not spoken about or seen. The *effects* of this subtext are seen – in the action. So with this particular writer I engage in a lot of brainstorming of the themes, the subtextual forces, contained in this one scene. The big question to ask is, 'How did we get here?' And the next one is, 'So what happens next?' The scene the writer has envisioned may be the end point of the whole series arc. It may actually, via much discussion, be in fact the midpoint of the series arc. Or, structured another way, it could be the jump off moment. What has to happen is that this scene becomes part of a longer and progressive sequence of subtextually driven story that results in travel, change and landing. All story is progression – which is why I use the process of story arcing throughout the work I do. The shape of that arc is by definition climbing, bending, coming to an apex and slewing down the other side to come to a rest point. The one scene is just an increment along that storyline.

ONE GREAT CONVERSATION

Yes, television stories must have relatable, energetic, popping dialogue. But it's not just about the words. In fact, in my world, it's about three essential layers working together and the words are part of one of those elements. There's nothing worse than turgid dialogue – it can bring a good script to its knees – but those words need visually backing up. So with the writer that brings me 'a series idea' that ultimately breaks down into 'One Great Conversation' I can at least have a strong start point. Here I spend a large amount of our development time drilling into the subtext of their key characters. What it is they want. What it is they fear. How they are going about getting what they want and what they – the writer – are doing about stopping them getting it. Desire vs Obstacle, to put it another way. Back to those three essential elements, which all good television writing has. They need to be contained in the series arc as a whole, in each episode as we break down that series arc incrementally, and then, pulling focus even more, in each scene of that episode.

They are: subtext, text and visual context. I will come back to these key areas in the next chapter on subtext, but I want to bring them up for discussion here, to drive home the concept that nothing in good television writing exists alone, in a vacuum. Emotional drive (subtext), plot (text) and visual context work together to make your series arc, your episode and your scene hit the spot we need it to with an audience. Put another way, the structure, the dialogue and the imagery you put together in a scene will bring the story and your message that bit closer to the heart of the series as a whole. You will be bringing it home. So, with this writer, I make sure that they can extrapolate outwards from this 'One Great Conversation' via the driving force of the character subtext. They can then wrap the action/plot (plus dialogue!) in a visual way to deliver an engaging series outline.

THE THING THAT HAPPENED TO ME

If you want to write the TV series of your life, or a key part of your life, start from character and make sure it's not you that sits in the centre of your story, but a character that represents you. The autobiographical, or semi-autobiographical, TV series is a landscape pitted with potholes (and plot holes!). I like working with a writer who brings to the development table a rich seam of story and experience taken from their memories and life lessons, but there are several danger areas to avoid. Firstly, and most importantly, many writers find it almost impossible to separate themselves and the people they remember from this time in their lives, from the story they want to tell. So we must begin the process by divorcing the writer from their personal connection, in order to truly deliver a commercial and creative project. Often I encourage writers to be economical with the actual truth of their experience – we are not in the business of reality TV or documentary after all – and in so doing, we can begin to fashion a story that has major influences in reality but is not a fly-on-the-wall take on the material. Often with a story of this nature I find the format length is a tricky thing to get right. As with most development work, we need to expand, extrapolate, build on the original experience to create enough 'narrative stretch'. I focus again on character here with the writer. It is by creating those crossover points within each of the characters' story arc that we begin to weave a drama dense enough to warrant a true series structure. Above all, we are making sure that this story is not, in fact, a single feature. Most times, I manage to create a series-arcing story from the writer's true experience, but there are times when the most we can effectively do is split the feature format into three and create a three-parter for TV.

In every case, it is important to allow the natural flow and shape of the story to take place and never to spread the storyline too thinly across the series for the sake of creating more episodes. Sometimes the best solution is to create a two- or three-parter. Make sure when you are working from a base of reality that you are not coming at this from a 'worthy' angle. No one likes well-meaning. Least of all producers. We are a cynical and story-hungry bunch.

Give us engagement, emotional attachment, connection, stakes, jeopardy and a strong climactic build up. Make the real part of the story as indiscernible from the truth as the made-up bits. Then we are talking proper immersion.

SUBTEXT: THE ESSENTIAL GUIDE

If you Google 'subtext', this comes up: 'An underlying and distinct theme in a piece of writing'. That's okayish... but not good enough. There's so much gubbins written about subtext. An internet trawl will take you down many a rabbit hole, and still there seems to be confusion amongst the writing community as to what subtext really is, and how it should be used in screenwriting. To my mind, subtext is an all-powerful narrative tool and the understanding of this and its uses in storytelling for television, forms the bedrock of the work I do with writers.

Subtext is the glue, the magic connective tissue, the membrane, the conduit, the binding agent of a great piece of writing. There is no good writing without subtext. There are no emotional, engaging, alluring, astonishing stories to tell without subtext. Plot alone is a vapid, empty shouting thing and all the action and bluster on the screen signifies nothing without the undertow – the driving force, the story engine chugging along underneath it all – of the subtext.

Marry subtext with text and message, and theme and What You Really Wanted To Say All Along will dance together, holding hands, at the wedding. So let's drill into how I see subtext and once you've grasped this notion, I guarantee your television writing will go up several notches. The writers whose work we love and admire – Russell T Davies, Michaela Coel, Sally Wainwright, Phoebe Waller-Bridge, Danny Brocklehurst, or Paul Abbott for example – all understand how subtext works and use it to the best effect in all their storytelling for the small screen.

In *Happy Valley*, Sally Wainwright created the central character of Catherine Cawood – Police Sergeant Community Officer and grieving mother, grandmother to her dead daughter's son. Her subtext punches through from below into everything she does, both personal and professional. She is an angry, frustrated, passionate, loving individual who, across series 2 (with series 3 currently transmitting on BBC1 at the time of writing this chapter) is coming to the end of her tether. Fighting her inner demons, she manages to put behind bars the rapist that killed her daughter and pick up the reins full time to parent her fractured grandchild. So here, and throughout the series, we see on screen how Catherine Cawood's subtext drives the story engine. It is her relentless pursuit of the man who killed her daughter and broke her own heart in the process that brings together the other series strands in this tour de force of television series writing. Subtext is then both a structural and an emotional tool writers use to highlight, orchestrate and deliver an overall arcing theme in a series, or a personal and powerful moment in a scene.

In my world, all good television scenes must include three essential layers forming the perfect drama terrine. Each work together with the others to create the perfect scenario. So, to recap...

Subtext – this punches in from below and is not spoken but seen and felt in a scene.

Text – this is the result of the subtext coming to the surface on screen. What we see is action, and what we know are plot points moving forward via this action but what we do not see but always feel is the subtext exerting its impact on the action.

Visual Context – an element of television writing some writers do not pay enough attention to. The subtext and the text form a symbiotic relationship in a scene, or a whole series strand. The visual used on the page and therefore on the screen, will somehow enhance, or contrast, highlight or clarify the message the scene is portraying to the audience.

Given television is a visual medium, subtext is not always felt in a scene because of the dialogue between two characters. Good dialogue is driven by subtext – what is driving the scene from the emotional point of view – but good television writing is a combination of dialogue, story structure and visual context. Subtext can be conveyed very powerfully by the visual alone.

In *Fleabag*, series 1 and 2, Phoebe Waller-Bridge writes from a visual outwards. She focuses her visual imagination in such a way that it engenders an emotional response. She is constantly channelling the subtext here. There are many examples in both series, but one visual in particular stands out from series 2. It's the last scene. Fleabag is walking away after saying goodbye forever to the priest she loves who cannot return that love. She is alone. London is dark and the streets are wet but she is at one with herself and her surroundings. She carries the statue she finally managed to get away from her manipulative stepmother. It is the figure this stepmother from Hell made herself, based on Fleabag's mother, and now, the rounded form sitting perfectly in her hand, Fleabag appears empowered, complete... almost happy.

All story development should start from subtext, not from plot. Characters make plot happen. Plot is not applied on top. Plot happens because of what is driving the character from within and how they are behaving as a result. The thinking is, 'What does my character want? Why do they want this? How are they going to get it? How can I stop that happening across the series arc?' To take a leaf out of Aaron Sorkin's book, I encourage my writers firstly to identify 'The Desire' of the character and then put 'An Obstacle' in the way of them attaining that. Rinse, repeat for the length of the series arc.

The thinking is not, 'I want my character to have an affair, get divorced, become a CEO, and miss her mother's funeral.' These things can happen, of course, but only when you have drilled down into what it is that is driving your character. These beliefs, emotions, fears and desires are the motor behind the narrative arc of your character. So once you have clarified what those drivers are, then your character can have an affair, which ends in divorce. The subtext driving this character could manifest as an overriding ambition as a consequence of which she attains the position of CEO against all odds. The knock-on effect of this behaviour results in estrangement or distraction to the point she misses her mother's funeral. All of your plot decisions are subtextually driven.

So the much shortened definition of subtext can be one word. Emotion. If you get confused or lost in the myriad definitions you find on the internet just go back to that one word. What is the emotional driver of your character? It is the ghost that you can't see that haunts your character. Everything they do is because of this subtext. Find out what that is and you will have your developing plot line.

The power and potency of subtext in good television writing cannot be understated. It can be:

Thematic – for example in Dan Erickson's unique and clever character-driven, high-concept piece *Severance*, the subtext is ever present via the visual conceit of the series as a whole and is the driving force behind every character due to the nature of the piece itself. The theme explores those that are severed from society and essentially why. Every plot point and character action is imbued with this underlying subtext of *Severance*. The theme holds the world and the story together and it is explored entirely by the use of subtext.

Visual – for example in Vince Gilligan/Bob Odenkirk's marvellous offshoot of *Breaking Bad*, *Better Call Saul*, the main character's office has fake Grecian pillars. As he makes his wife wait in the antechamber to sign the papers for a divorce which he doesn't want to happen, he accidentally knocks one of the pillars down. The falling fake pillars make a subtextual comment on his life, his work and the man he is allowing himself to become.

Structural – subtext brings together themes, storylines and the series throughline of the whole piece – it is the linking agent in all the layers of the narrative on screen.

Emotional – the 'not said' part of good subtextually driven dialogue makes the spoken words clearer and carry more weight. For example, Kim Wexler in *Better Call Saul* listens on the phone to her ex-husband Saul Goodman aka Jimmy McGill and attempts to get a word in sideways whilst he reprimands her for not sticking by him. She lets him vent. Then she says, 'I am glad you are alive' and quickly puts the phone down. The audience know she still feels for him but knows he can't be helped and that she is tortured by this.

Dynamic – working with text, subtext creates narrative energy on screen and drives the scene forward. Subtext makes you a better writer. When writers feel the need to fill in the gaps in the dialogue with more words and suffocate the potential emotional undertow punching in from below, subtext dies and exposition rears its ugly head. This is the rotting agent of good writing. Let subtext breathe life into your writing.

So in answer to the question 'What is subtext?' I say subtext is *Everything.*

LET'S DISCUSS... **THE PILOT**

As a writer, you should, in my view, also be a reader. I read a lot of scripts because of the work I do, but I also enjoy reading scripts as a way not only to keep tabs on who's writing what but also on how they're doing it.

There's a few rules of thumb that I give to my writers when it comes to writing and formatting your scripts for television – and many of these you will be familiar with as they are all over the internet and in general parlance everywhere within the industry. Two of the most oft quoted are: 'Show, Don't Tell' and 'Less Is More'. And then the fabulous, instinctive, inspiring writers such as Sally Wainwright go ahead and ignore those rules – which you will find if you read any of her work online. She loves a strong and often long scene description, for example. So obviously I proceed with caution here, but suffice to say, if you keep your work visual and you are succinct where you really need to be, then you won't go far wrong.

You will, if you are following my process, have already expanded and developed your key character arcs so you will know where each character starts their story along their timeline and in general the big arcing themes for them. You will know where you imagine their series midpoint will be and how they will land in the series at the end. So you will be in a good position to have now mapped out what is in the pilot itself and written what I call a Pilot Map. This is a scene-by-scene breakdown of the hour you intend to sell the rest of the series. Again a rule of thumb: 60 pages for a television hour, 30 pages for a television half hour. One minute per page. Always write to the full hour. Your work, once commissioned, will be cut into and shaped by the slot and the broadcaster or streamer in question. It will invariably shrink so write to the roundest representation of the story that you can.

The pilot has a big responsibility. It needs to be a precursor for the rest of the series, and producers/readers need to be able to glean from the tone, the plot and the characterisation what they can expect in the series going forward.

THE ESSENTIAL FIVE ELEMENTS FOR A STRONG COMMERCIAL PILOT

1. OPEN WITH A STRONG VISUAL

The story is starting so set the scene.

Geography – be it a panoramic landscape or a cosy tête-à-tête in a suburban sitting room, a graveside, a rooftop, or the inside of a rapidly packed suitcase – begins the story for you.

You may need to establish the way a character behaves, or show the essential dynamic within a family. Do this visually. This visual can be a strong natural image, or series of images. It can be an action-packed travelling sequence or we could be following your main character on the job. But in this visual, we need to see the essential elements of what you will be exploring later on in the pilot and series.

Start the audience wondering what's going to happen.

Examples of visual starts in scripts, picked as randomly as possible:

Rooftops of a Northern town. We pick up a central character putting the bins out. They look up and we see what they see – their ex-wife doing the same. They stare across the cobbles at each other. *Coronation Street*.

Windswept moorland and a galloping horse. A man is riding very fast and we can be pretty sure the place he's going will be where the next bit of the story will start, so we are keen for him to get there. *Poldark*.

A man stands in a desert in his underpants. He is holding a gun. There's a Winnebago next to him. It looks very hot out there and he is clearly upset. *Breaking Bad*.

Two elderly people in a café. Quintessentially English. Their conversation soon encompasses their respective spouses and offspring. At first they appear to be strangers but soon we realise they are actually flirting. *Last Tango in Halifax*.

The back garden of a local house in rural Yorkshire and a grumpy cop realises there's nothing she can do about the mauled sheep found dying on the nice old lady's neatly mowed lawn. She accepts a cup of tea and, when the lady pops back to her kitchen, she staves the sheep's head in with a brick. *Happy Valley*.

A jaded journalist is a reluctant part of a discussion panel for a room full of young journalists and students on the nature of America and its place in world politics. He sees his ex in the audience with a prompt card. He decides to tell the truth. *The Newsroom*.

2. CRACK INTO CHARACTER

Every second counts on the screen so translate that directly to the page and make everything that a character does and says in the first ten pages mean something. Motivate every word they say from their subtext. You have to know your character really well to be able to do this with conviction. The subtexts of this character and those around them will push the narrative forward. It's not only what a character says which will give us important information about them, it's how they say it. So remember the action; 'see' how your characters move and interact. Everything a character does with their body will say something about their character. Having said that, please don't overstate this direction in your script.

3. START THE PLOT MOVING

The subtext is deep and solid in all your characters (of course!), so you will have no problem moving the plot forward. But it is essential that you keep up the rhythm here. In the first ten pages the plot – or text, motivated by the subtext of your characters – must reach a point whereby your audience/reader will want to get to the next ten minutes (roughly ten pages). So you need to set up the main frame of your story in these pages and also introduce a twist, or an added point of happy writing engagement.

4. SET UP THE DESIRED GOAL

All your characters want something, so set this up in the first ten pages. This is their jump off point. Then aim for their midpoint in the series arc, generating enough energy in the pilot to get them there.

5. ADD THE OPPOSITION TO THAT GOAL

The truth, and therefore the point of dramatic engagement from both your reader and ultimately your audience, will come from the interplay between what your character wants and how you, the writer, chooses to stop them getting it.

Always write from the truth and 'If you've lived, don't make stuff up!' – Tony Jordan on writers over 40.

To those of you who are not even rounding the bend of that particular curve, fear not: the message is the same.

Write from your own personal centre of truth.

We all have emotions, conceits, ideas and mantras that we follow in life. Things that matter to us. A way of seeing and interpreting the world. And that is what the industry wants. Writers need to tap into that complex, dense, often not very savoury centre of 'us' and then the story unfolds in a truthful way. Then the real connections can be made between those that create these scenarios for our screens and those that watch them.

It's an all-round activity, watching drama on the big and small screens. When we engage with a story we are doing so with our logical brains and with our hearts. We understand something we are being told rationally but we also react most viscerally to how that story makes us feel.

Writers are in the business of bringing that 360-degree experience to the audience. So if you don't personally feel it, they won't. Tap into what you know about your world. Not what you think we want to know.

Having written what I rather horribly call the 'Vomit Draft' of your pilot and reminding yourself of the wisdom of Paul Abbott when he said 'All writing is rewriting', you now begin the process of going back over it all and rewriting what didn't quite work first time. So get stuck in.

Firstly, check the page count. If you find your pilot is running more than a couple of minutes over at this early stage, the chances are you are either not ending the pilot at the best point for the overall story, or that somewhere you are overwriting. Or it could be that scenes aren't delivering the punch they need to, in which case there may be a certain amount of redundancy at this point.

Then try and take an overall view, flicking through the pages, so that you get a sense of what the text looks like on the page. If there are chunky blocks of text, if there are dense, over-long passages spoken by one character, if it is static and verbose, warning bells should begin to ring. You are aiming all the time to move the story visually and with energy – think of dialogue as a flowing, travelling thing that goes down the page and doesn't stagnate for any length of time.

Overly wordy or didactic passages are the narrative form of strychnine, and they are also extremely dull to watch on screen. Keep it all moving. If your pilot has a lot of these blocky moments, my gut feeling is that you are forgetting the visual aspect of the medium you're writing for, and also you may have forgotten the audience. Always keep in mind that macro viewpoint of the audience vs the micro viewpoint of the characters in your world, and the need to keep flipping from one perspective to another to keep the narrative flowing and the story engine moving everything along. If you can, try to respond instinctively to your own writing. Does this engage? Entertain? Do you want to know what happens next?

I recently asked Tony Jordan, CEO of Red Planet Pictures and a series drama powerhouse, about script editors, and he said this; 'My relationship with a script editor is the most important creative relationship I have in television. The good ones make me a better writer.'

The years that I have accumulated in script editing and developing the scripted word – so many hours of script reading – have meant that often I am instinctive, almost knee-jerk, about aspects of the work I read on the page. If the flow of the storyline is not sufficiently controlled or if the structure of the script is undermined by poor choices regarding its shape, then, as I read it, something will jar and stop me turning the page. I always then refer back to the structure of the work.

Structure really is the beginning, the middle and the end of truly good writing. Without a solid, supportive framework, your story will not shine and your script will not be successful. So make your structural decisions early on. How are you going to tell your story and who carries the main weight of your narrative? Or is this an ensemble piece? Make sure you know (because you have plotted all the arcs before you start your script) where the various storylines of your characters intercut or impact on each other. This is where you will find most engagement from your script editor and then, by extension, your audience. Reading your own work is an exposing and necessary part of your development process. You are now your own script editor. These are the areas I suggest you pay most attention to with your script editor hat on.

Text (the plot: what is happening, what is action) and subtext (the motivation: what drives a character, what is suggested, not stated) are the dramatic siblings to look at next. This is because your analysis of the structural issues will inevitably overlap with your consideration of text and subtext. As you're reading the script, be aware of the storyline, noting how it is being pushed through the script, but always keeping a tab on the subtext – that motivational force behind each scene.

Subtext and text will have a dramatic impact on the next area you will need to address: another often warring coupling, dialogue and characterisation. When addressing the dialogue in a script, make sure you don't make the mistake of allowing the subtext to poke through the spoken word on the page. When a character literally speaks their subtext (for example: 'Being here like this, with you, makes me feel uncomfortable') this is too on the nose. Lean into the subtext when you write any scene and most importantly throughout the pilot. When the subtext isn't there, it all becomes about the text, that's when Exposition rears its ugly head. Avoid it.

It is also important to handle the overall pacing in the script right through from scene 1 to FADE OUT. There is a natural flow to storylines if handled correctly, and scripts that stand up to the description 'page turner' do not need to contain high-octane, high-impact action scenes from beginning to end. Obviously there needs to be something going on, but action doesn't have to be an explosion or a physical stunt. An audience can be very effectively held by drawing on pure emotion that comes from the subtext. The script needs to answer to the internal metronome of the storyline. Some have a gentler beat than others. The key is to mix it up a bit and not allow your work to level out and flatline.

WHERE'S **THE ARC?**

Often writers come to me with 'the whole thing' in their head or as an outline on paper. This is the summary of the series they want to write but presented in a solid unit of story that has more in common with a feature than a series. This is also because invariably this story has been conceived with a three-act structure – put simply, a beginning, a middle and an end. My job is to extrapolate from the main body of this story the series strands that are potentially revealing themselves.

I need to create Narrative Stretch. We need to front load the story in the beginning of the series arc. So we drill into the subtext of the characters that we have identified sit in the centre of the story. In that small circle of the bicycle wheel – central to the world portrayed and instrumental in the flow of storyline from the middle outwards. Creating connection points, crossovers and junctions between the storylines of the centrally positioned characters gives more story. The more this happens in Act One of the pilot, the better the chances of pulling out the fabric of the story across the series.

It's all about creating a strong series core at the outset, so you know exactly what is underlying the story as a whole and what your exploration of this underlying core will bring to the series: a cohesion and a consistent tension for your audience throughout the arc of the series. Consider the core of *Detectorists* (Mackenzie Crook/ BBC1/Netflix) – which I consider to be a masterclass in how to generate story from character subtext and connection. The core – or to put it another way, the narrative throughline – is all about finding gold. The business of metal detecting. What it means to consistently walk in lines through ploughed fields, waving your detector in an endless arc, listening for the beep that indicates a find.

This also sets the tone of the series. It is a thing of gentle observation, of moments strung together by virtue of the fact that the act of metal detecting takes time and application and a repeat of the same behaviour. It takes endurance. And here there are no big stunts, no wild accusations and no high drama. Here there is constancy, repetition, a connection between characters begun by their mutual love of the art of metal detecting but continued through their wider connections in the community in which they live, and the relationships they form. The tone is what separates it from other dramas. There is an exaggerated edge to some of the characters here (notably the rival detectorists our boys wryly name Simon and Garfunkel) but none of this is two-dimensional – the characterisation is key and real for everyone.

In the series arc of *Detectorists*, the core is strong because the series intent is clear. This is about the 'hobby' or 'art' or 'obsession' that is metal detecting and the people that love it. It is about how ordinary people can, through endurance and diligence (skills not celebrated in this modern day of get-rich-quick and immediate returns) make extraordinary things happen.

There is an obvious structural connection between the characters in this perfectly formed series. Here we, the macro view, can observe their quiet battles, their inner demons at work, whilst they lay out their 'treasure' on the Finds Table at their weekly meetings. We may judge them for their parochial behaviour, this small, rather silly thing they do, but we are also drawn into the day-to-day magic of being a detectorist with a soul, as we become invested in the lives of Andy and his best mate Lance.

There is a dual progression to the structure of *Detectorists*. First, there is the relationship on which the series essentially focuses – Andy and Lance's friendship and their personal growth as people. Second, there is the thematic link to the title *Detectorists* which invites us to consider the ethos of a detectorist – what makes a good one – and how by following this discipline, you can, with a good heart and the right work ethic, find gold, both in terms of friendship and love, and also the shiny hard stuff.

Identifying the arc of both character (in terms of motivation, subtext and text) and the series arc as a whole is the most important part of television drama development in my book. Once you've found the arc, then the business of building on that and creating more connection, more extension in the storyline can begin. One of the most frequent mistakes made in plotting and mapping a series arc is that too much story can be applied too soon and then the series feels top-heavy. The other mistake is the opposite problem, when too much story has been withheld for too long and the series arc is bottom-heavy. And then there's the issue of not enough story which is spread too thinly across the arc. So it's an issue of distribution. But creation first, then the mapping begins.

I like to brainstorm as much as possible with my writers at the outset. Really drill into character and then, once we have what feels like enough strands for each of the main characters in the wheel, we can start pulling these out into episodes and begin the process of the arcing of the series. Have a general idea of where you want the series to land as you do this arcing, so you are aiming at something. The key to storylining/creating strong arcs is to keep in mind the jump off, the midpoint and the landing of each character's story as they go through the series. Then you can also see how each storyline can create more tension by the weaving of those storylines across and through each other. Characters will form groupings or duos that work storywise for you. In the developmental process you will start to see who these people are and who best they are teamed with to make the drama tick.

And the other key thing to remember when creating series arcs is my 'Rule of Three'. Seed. Explore. Payoff. This applies to the character arcs as you develop the journey of your key players, and also the series arc as a whole, when you've brought all the players together. So starting wide, we look at the series arc as a bigger picture. We see that the first part of the arc is where the story is seeded. The midpoint comes when we have expanded the themes and the storylines into a climactic midway point in the overall arc. The latter part of the series is all about bringing those storylines to a landing point, to payoff in the last episode.

AND SO TO **THE PITCH...**

There's a lot to unpack around the concept of pitching. Organised, planned-for pitching is a different creature than spontaneous, this-thing-is-happening-without-my-prior-knowledge pitching. And group pitching is a totally different situation on every level to a one-on-one pitch. There's an awkward frisson between informal and formal to a pitch that brings with it its own rather delightful energy. This thing feels natural, but could go horribly wrong. It's a fine line the pitcher and pitchee are walking here. In my experience, it's better to be pitched at than to be the one doing the pitching. Although being the pitchee has its own particular burdens too.

I have sat in various offices at Granada Television and at the BBC, when I was a development script editor for the series department of both broadcasters, and listened, with growing concern (and trying for it not to show on my face), as the writer across the desk from me tried to extricate themselves from the morass of words they had managed to get mangled into – like a fish gasping in a net of misfiring sentences and false starts. Then a space within the wordage appears and I manage to say something that (hopefully) takes the edge off the situation and allows them either to start again or continue with less angst.

Pitching can happen on the hoof – literally 'walking and talking' to the lift of a building you might find yourself in with the producer you want to see. This could be at a Screen Festival or event, or a meet and greet. This has happened to me. It's nerve-racking but when your key guy or gal says, 'Let's walk and talk', they don't mean, 'Let's chat about this and that and the latest episode of *Married at First Sight'* – although these are perfectly good opening conversations to the big one if the mood feels right.

They mean, 'Tell me about your project. I am showing enough interest to get us to the lift, and you have about two minutes to get this across.' When an improvised pitch looks like a possibility, focus on the Rule of Three. Seed. Explore. Payoff. You introduce the conceit. You expand a bit on the main throughline and then you pay it off with a rounded couple of sentences that both tie up the earlier seeding, but also suggest further action. Improvised pitches need practising as much as the ones you have planned for.

Pitching a story when you are a writer on an established show and attending the story conference regularly through the production year is a specific and exacting art. You are laying out your story on the table, as it were, showing the components to the wider group of your fellow writers (who are also pretty focused on voicing their own stories for the show they really want to keep writing for) and to your bosses, the producers or executive producers, who need to feel confident in their belief in you as part of this writing stable and in your ability to provide story ideas to feed their eternally hungry series monster. No one actually says it, but story conference is a time when the writing team needs to shine at all costs. It's the best fun and the worst too, all at the same time.

Not every writer thrives at story conference – those with personalities that are more introvert than extrovert, for instance, tend to dread it more than the ones that are naturally vocal and perhaps more experienced in this part of the production process on a long runner. In my experience, the quieter writers around the table may not get the earlier chances to pitch but the executive running the conference will note this and hopefully give them a chance to present something. It's definitely the accepted thing to make sure everyone gets a go at addressing the room. At the end of the day, story production is a collaborative process and the production needs the writers' input like they do oxygen on a show that literally eats story.

Pitching to a producer or script executive on your own feels very different. Although in a group setting there's competition, there's also a particular and usually very strong camaraderie between your fellow writers; and this glue is often what helps stick your pitch together if it goes a bit pear-shaped. Here, going solo, there's no support. The sound of your own voice, perhaps sounding too loud in the room, is all you have to focus on as you launch into the hopefully pithy sell of your story to the person that said they wanted to hear about it.

I used to regularly pitch to the ITV network on behalf of Granada Television and the drama series department. Sometimes these pitches would go so well I was convinced I'd made a certain sale and then we wouldn't hear for ages until we did get a definite no. Sometimes I knew from the start my pitch was doomed. One particular time is still etched in my memory. I had, the day before Pitch Day, rather ill-advisedly moved flat and had spent much of the previous night drinking wine with my bestie. On the morning of the Pitch, I realised I had packed all my clothes in boxes which were currently stacked like the last scene in *Raiders of the Lost Ark*, going back in perspective from the bedroom door to the front door. With the clock ticking and time running out, I scanned the debris of my room and spied a pair of trousers and a tee shirt sticking out of a bin bag. Easy. I put them on and made a run for the door. Putting my make-up on in the taxi going to ITV Network Centre that morning, I realised to my horror that my trousers were shiny disco pants – metallic in fact – and that my tee shirt was cut low and had a stain right in the middle of it – like a medal (think it was soy sauce) between my breasts. Nightmare. I looked like a ginger version of Bubble from *Ab Fab*. Nick Elliot was Controller of the ITV Network at the time and he was very nice about this rag-taggle vision with badly applied mascara and dubious stain. I don't remember much about the actual pitch – I was far too distracted by what I am sure was an alarming appearance – but, suffice to say, he didn't go for the series.

I know some writers love to pitch, but the majority I find do not. The best pitches are, to my mind, the ones that aren't planned. The most successful pitches I have ever managed to pull off are the ones where the conversation is easy and you feel confident of your territory. You need to really feel the veracity of your story – truly believe in it. And it does help, in my experience, to be able to say, 'It's a bit like X crossed with Y but not exactly...' Comparisons are good because they are a shortcut to getting to your show without having to do too much set-up beforehand. Producers like to feel they are going to get something that is a bit like... *(insert successful show of your choice)*... but isn't that. They would very much like the Same, only Different.

It's a lottery. But don't lose before you start by using rambling, unnecessary detail. Avoid diversions from the main throughline of your story. Identify that before you get in the room – way before – and stick to the plan of delivery. Don't deviate. Practise the pitch at home. Out loud. Time it. Be an actor here. Eye contact is key too. Don't overdo it. I once got so carried away pitching to a respected but rather tricky producer (known for their inattentiveness) that I found myself perched on the edge of his desk by the time I had finished my pitch. Getting myself off his desk, and into the chair I was meant to be sitting in, took an ungainly and protracted number of moves that I really wish I hadn't had to do in a pencil skirt.

The game here is to get the person in question interested enough, not only to take the treatment from your outstretched hand, but also to ask for the pilot script. So I advise you to have written the script before you start getting the opportunity to pitch. The worse scenario is the producer likes the sound of your pitch – you didn't mess up – they ask if you have a script they could read and you don't have it ready. They will give you a window of a few weeks before the heat goes off the initial pitch and you've lost the opportunity. I wouldn't advise trying to write a cracking pilot in a few weeks even if you have followed all my structural process and you have it mapped and outlined.

So bite the bullet. Pitching is a necessary evil and it's just one of those things you have to do to get your work out there and discussed. We are in the business, after all, of exchanging ideas, stories, experiences and for producers/

commissioners, this is their lifeblood. Content, as Tony Jordan has said, is King.

So, now you have that very content. You've worked for months on this thing and you are ready, because you have done the structure, the writing and the rewriting work, to let your story out into the big wide open air. There's a pressure. There's an expectation. On both sides. There's a time limit. You know you can't mess this up. There's a small window of opportunity just opened and you are desperate you won't snag your story knickers trying to squeeze through it.

But here's what you know. You know what the essence of your television project is. You know what the central message is within it. You know who your world revolves around. You know what they do and why they do it. You have a framework. You may not have written all the documents I outline below, but to begin the conversation with confidence you will have written a strong treatment which you will be aiming to leave with the producer you're chatting with now. And to whet their whistle you may have sent them, in your email, your one-pager so they know the general territory of the idea that you are here to discuss.

These are the stages of the producer conversation you may have following your pitch as represented by key television documents. They are also discussed in Chapters 4 and 5 but I lay them out here because they are key both to a structurally commercial series and to a creative conversation about that series:

ONE-PAGER – A succinct, visual, engagingly written summary of the story and its main throughline featuring the key characters and a sense of the tone and themes held within it.

THE TREATMENT – Increasingly longer in length as each TV year goes by, but still I suggest no more than 10 text pages (excluding imagery), which breaks down the DNA of your series as a whole. Crucially, at this point of a pitch you will be needing a strong, relevant logline that you can learn, which you will make sure forms a key part of your treatment.

THE SERIES OUTLINE – Again, try to keep this as succinct as possible. Producers want to see the general flow of the episodes across the arc of the series. They do not want dialogue, too much detail or 'he said, she said' scenarios – but they do want engaging, visual, short summaries of what each episode contains, so at a glance and without much effort, they can visualise the rest of the series as it flows from the pilot episode.

A CRACKING PILOT – It goes without saying that this has to be strong, characterful and display your 'voice' in its best light. It needs to have pace, tone, be robust visually and have a story engine that motors from the first minute to the last. Within the time span of your pilot you will need to have created at least one strong 'peak' of action (motivated by subtext) in each of the five acts that split up your dramatic timeline. A strong midpoint and an attention-grabbing, interesting end point with which to hook into episode 2. (For more detail refer to Chapter 8)

TEMPLATE FOR A
TELEVISION TREATMENT

Over the years of working with writers from the point of view of firstly a script editor, then a producer, then an executive producer and now a script consultant, I can honestly say that although this is not rocket science by any shape or form, my treatment template really does help break down the DNA of the series you want to create for television. I put this together because I know what a producer is looking for when it comes to a new idea and I also know how the writer brain works – in the creation of your world you mustn't get lost and lose focus. So this document, simplistic maybe, but effective definitely, is what I use to help writers and ultimately producers get to grips with the next TV series idea.

TITLE – Make yours really sell your idea by being the best you can make it. But titles are not just about the selling angle – they are, in my book, essential to maintaining the tone and structure of the storytelling throughout the series arc. Titles hold the essence of the idea within them and they form the series narrative throughline. It is by recalling and referring to the title throughout your writing of the series that you will ensure you always keep the main narrative drive to the forefront of your mind as well as the tone of the whole piece. Examples of good titles that do all of the above are: *Happy Valley*; *The Good Wife*; *Succession*; *Peaky Blinders*; *Hacks*; *Bad Sisters*.

FORMAT DESCRIPTION – These are the definitions that describe my working day and most of my television career in drama production. Series: A drama that is open-ended. A core cast of returning characters. The backdrop remains the same and is returned to each week. This is also called 'the Precinct'. There may be several stories per episode which are resolved, but the series storyline, that which is carried by the core returning cast, remains open. For example: *Ozark*, *Coronation Street*, *Ghosts*, *Unforgotten*, *Skins*. Serial or miniseries: A drama of more than two parts with a strong serial element. A core cast of returning characters and an over-arcing storyline, but in this case the storyline is ultimately resolved. For example: *Chernobyl*, *Unbelievable*, *The Queen's Gambit*, *Unorthodox*, *The Gilmore Girls*, and *Nine Perfect Strangers*. Here in your treatment you state how long your series or serial is x 3/4/6/8 parts. Or is it a series of 13 or more parts?

LOGLINE – In a paragraph, short enough to memorise but long enough to say what you need it to, summarise your idea as succinctly and entertainingly as you can. You need to convey the main narrative here – the set-up, the jeopardy or challenge for your character/s – and to give a sense of style and tone by the way you word this. This is what your producer/commissioner will keep referring to in your conversation about the drama and its future development. A couple of examples…

Behind the glossy facade of this luxury hotel franchise, lurks the dark underbelly of the human condition. Here greed, lust and avarice run riot amongst the pampered guests whilst those that serve them fight their own inner demons. Not so much resort as moral boot camp, this holiday comes at a high price which you could pay for with not just your cash, but your life. *The White Lotus*.

Yorkshire is God's Own Country but threading through the green fells and quaint villages is a dark seam of unemployment, poverty, drug addiction and gang warfare. In the middle sits Catherine Cawood, a granny, a grieving mum, a dutiful sister and a very good police sergeant to boot. She has put her nemesis, the man she holds responsible for the death of her daughter, behind bars and she's not going to take any more shit. *Happy Valley*.

ONE PARAGRAPH OF TASTY DESCRIPTION SETTING OUT THE WORLD – Here the job is to be as descriptive and evocative as possible. Imagine you are telling your friend about a film you have just seen that truly made an impact on you. You need to entice them into the storyline, to make them want to see it too. Use your internal eye and set out some key visual moments. They need not be the first ones seen in the first scene of your pilot, but they could be set pieces (as discussed in Chapter 1) by which I mean a sequence of scenes that is driven from beneath by subtext. This then reveals the text on screen (plot) and is delivered in a visual way to further reflect the narrative throughline – or title. Visualise and describe for us what is going on. Draw us in.

CHARACTER ARCS – I don't refer to these just as Character Biographies, because they are more than that. In my world, the treatment will always explore the potential storyline arcs for every character in the series. So here, you need to map out in very broad strokes and as succinctly as possible, the general overarching storyline for each individual character. It helps to put a three- or four-line paragraph at the end of each character arc, to sum up what their main challenge is, what they learn and how they are changed by it. You do not need to be exact here – you don't need to blow the whole plot line if there are surprises in store – but tease/ engage the reader by suggestion, and allude to the main story engine for each character. The idea here is to give the potential producer a strong idea of where the story is going for each character so they begin to build up a picture of the series as a whole.

SUMMARY OF EPISODE ONE – Here a producer needs to know the general flow and content of the story and understand how the story unfolds via your characters' arcs in the pilot. Cover the main dramatic connections, how your characters interact and the outcome of the plot line. Make this an engaging, visual read – help them 'see' the pilot in their mind's eye.

EPISODE OUTLINES – Be exact and succinct in your language. Avoid, 'then she said, then he said' (which is oxygen-sucking for anyone to read). There is a traditional method of story structure used notably in soaps and the longer-running, open-ended dramas – that of the A, B, C, D storyline structure. This is a very good way to structure soaps or open-ended series which often carry large amounts of narrative and, as a result, have bigger casts. If this is a method you are using, make sure that your A storyline sits at the centre of each of your episode summaries and then weave the B and C etc. around that. If you are not structuring in this way, then summarise here the main thrust of the episode from the point of view of the characters that carry the most narrative weight. The key here is to keep the producer engaged whilst ensuring the summary pushes the narrative forward both visually and from an emotional point of view.

The reason the episodes are here in the treatment is to prove to a prospective buyer/producer that your idea really does warrant the episodes you say you are aiming for. So, if there are 6 parts or 10, a producer will be looking at whether there is enough story material to go the distance. Some producers may ask for more detail at this point, and you can then provide them with a step-by-step breakdown of the story as it unfolds in each episode. Here, in the treatment, you are setting out the long arcs – the broad strokes – and you need to give an impression of plenty but avoid tedious details.

THE CENTRAL MESSAGE – This will most likely be alluded to in your logline, but here you can extrapolate a bit more and dig a bit deeper. What do you want your audience to come away thinking, having spent time with your drama? What is it you are saying about the world and your characters? What is the macro message to be gleaned from diving, as we have done here in your treatment, into the micro world of your drama?

HOW TO WORK WITH **KEY PLAYERS**

Television drama development through to production is very much a team effort. Yes, of course, there's the solitary writer at the beginning of the process but you have to get your stories out into the world very soon after you've got them out of you. And this is often the really hard part. It's exposing to have your work – the stuff of your soul – read by people with whom you will often only have a fledgling relationship. But that's where the good stuff can start. Your work may be the beginning of a collaboration between yourself and a potential producer and their company. So try and keep your ego at the door once you have had a favourable response to your one-pager, treatment or script from the people who could make it all happen, and focus on the job in hand.

A PRODUCTION COMPANY

Working with a production company is a bit like being in a romantic relationship without the sex. It can all start very well. They love your series. They think you are brilliant. Your initial meetings are full of praise for your writing. And you seem to have so much in common: the mutual love of similar shows, the mutual dislike of other shows. There may initially be small talk but, as the meetings become more frequent, the formality can begin to fade until you feel like you are working now with people who really 'get' you. Try and manage this stage carefully. There's a connection here, yes, but the continuance of this love affair is dependent on the progress of the project, the working practice in place and your ability to be flexible whilst also holding true to your heart the future of the project in question.

Production companies love to have solid, interesting, exciting, creative and commercial projects on their slates but they are not in the business of paying out for work that does not meet their criteria and once you are 'in conversation' with them, they will want to ensure you deliver their vision. They love you and your work but they have criteria in their remit that you may not be aware of. They need to make sure you can deliver the series you first discussed in your honeymoon period of meetings. Are you on the same page? When the changes start to happen, when the notes get more detailed and become longer or more frequent, and you feel you're having to try that much harder to keep the relationship fresh, that is the time to take a cleansing breath and dig deep.

Do not rush in, promising the world and then having sleepless nights and chronic heartburn for weeks afterwards, when you realise the work you said you can do in the time, you actually can't. There's a delicate balance to be created here between being available, able and enthusiastic about reworkings, rewrites and changes to your original piece (because inevitably there will be many of them) and protecting the initial vision of what you wanted to write in the first place.

The chances are, if you are this far down the development path with a production company, that you have an agent who can diplomatically handle your corner here. However, in my experience, writers are increasingly getting to this stage (often with my help, or that of someone like me) without an agent. The reason they are in this lucky (if sometimes tricky) position is that their script has done the talking for them. Producers are very hungry for great content in these days of fragmentation and multi-platforms. Although the business is more competitive than when I first started in it 30 years ago, now is actually a fantastic time to be a talented writer, even without an agent.

Gone are the days when an agent was the only way you would ever get seen or read by a production company. Now, increasingly, I am finding that, if your work is strong enough and if you have what they want, a production company will see you without representation. Often too, the production company may suggest agents for you because you do need legal and commercial support when your series takes off. Everyone wants to feel they are represented, and that the process you're involved in is fair. Agents, from both the production company's and the writer's point of view, give that reassurance.

The ethos and working environment within a production company invariably reflect those of their original founders/ CEOs. You may not meet or work directly with the CEOs but the development executive that you are working with will mirror the opinions and needs of their bosses. In some cases this can lead to a very easy, almost laidback way of working and, in others, you may find yourself in a much more frenetic and highly-charged environment.

The key here is to hold your ego to account but remain grounded, if you can, in your own belief in your work and in the reason they are taking this time to help you shape your vision for their purposes. It may feel like you are being moulded and that your original series is also being changed as a result. The answer here is to separate yourself, the writer – the creative force – from the work itself. I know this is hard. But remember again, this is a collaborative process. You can't make television without a team and you need this team to get your work out there. You need them. They need you. Ideally this is a symbiotic relationship and no one is getting their blood sucked.

Most production companies worth their salt have excellent, diplomatic, empathetic script development teams, whose job it is to make your work shine under their logo and to also bring out the best in you, as an individual creative. It's a fabulous position to be in for you and your work. So embrace the changes, and take the various atmospheric pressures you may encounter on the chin.

I don't want to be too prescriptive here, in regard to the stages of script development you may encounter when working with a production company. Suffice to say, you will either have written a one-pager or a treatment which has got you through the door and started the conversation with the company in question. After a couple of general development chats with the script editor/executive, in which you subliminally work out whether you could work together (leave that ego behind here, remember!), you may reach the option stage. Your work will be optioned for a period of time (six months or a year usually) and you will be paid an option for the company to take this on to their books and develop it as they see fit for the market they have in mind. Your job is to facilitate this development by representing your voice, your tone and your message within the parameters of the company that has effectively bought your series idea (as represented by the treatment or one-pager you wrote) for the duration of the option.

If your access to the production company and its development process started with them reading your pilot script of the series, then they will be required to buy this script from you and pay for an option of whatever period is agreed, in order to make any changes from this point onwards. They will then be legally within their rights to shape this script to fit the rigours of the pilot they wish to produce. Or it may be that the series arc is also under discussion and the script you wrote actually doesn't fit their vision for the pilot – it is in fact, in their minds, episode 2, for example.

Depending on your level of experience, it may be that you will not be required to write the pilot episode. If another, more experienced writer is brought in, then again you need to dig deep and allow this not to be the reason you walk away. You may be able to negotiate a place on the writing team for later episodes down the line. You may find it better all round to take a script consultant role and be part of the writers' room, or you may decide to take a back seat in the writing of your series but ensure you have 'created by' credits, even if you don't end up with a 'written by' credit. And again, the production company will ensure you are paid a format fee (typically an agreed percentage of the production budget attached to the project) for the series that was created by you and brought to them initially.

There are many stages between the first developmental conversation and the green light – the key is to keep a clear head and your feet on the ground. This is about getting your work out there and adopting a strong, resilient mindset will give you the best opportunity to do just that, forming healthy working relationships with key players along the way.

A WRITERS' ROOM

Increasingly the UK development landscape mirrors that of the established system in the US and features writers' rooms. These are a way of generating long-running series using the core group of writers that have been brought in by the producers to work up the series arcs and beat out the episodic storylines for the characters, across the duration of the series. Usually confronted with a white board, and often headed up by the showrunner of the piece (who will often be the series creator as well as the lead writer), writers' rooms are the engine room of the series machine. The work is intense and focused over a specific development period (again dictated by the amount of run-up time on the prospective show). If/when the series is commissioned, this team will go forward to write the transmitted episodes.

There's a hierarchy here, in that there will be a lead writer or perhaps a writing duo that will lead the thrust of the story discussion and keep the energy of the sessions flowing. Like in any good story conference on established series, there will be an expectation to contribute positively and with a 'can do' mindset to the overall story wall that you will be party to constructing.

There will be lots of discussions around storyline, character, series intent, mood and tone and ultimately these conversations will need to be brought to a strong conclusion within the deadline set by the executive producer.

The writers' room is the crucible of story creation and development for the series and, as a result, you will have a significant amount of responsibility in terms of generating storylines with enough drive and layering to create the strongest series possible. You will also be required to work with several other writers, all of whom bring their own 'take' and personality to the table. It is the job of the showrunner to create a harmonious working practice but your job to be part of that harmony and ensure you are good to work with.

A SCRIPT EXECUTIVE/CONSULTANT

Working with a script consultant or script editor is not something every freelance writer in the early stages of their career will need. In fact, I suggest that unless you have been concentrating on your writing for at least a year – reading, watching shows and pushing out your scripts – you won't actually benefit from working with a professional script editor. You need to have gained in both maturity and experience as a writer before the skills and process of a script editor or consultant will be able to truly help you raise your writing bar.

Use a script consultant to help you shape your projects professionally for market, to increase your exposure to the industry via production companies and/or agents who are in their orbit, and to get used to working collaboratively on your projects with an outside eye. The risk for a writer working solo and without representation at this point is that they may become insular, out of touch with the industry and actually write more of their project than is needed or even healthy for their own state of mind. As I said at the beginning of this book, you need to get your work out there as soon as you feel it and you are ready. Using a script consultant or script editor who has contacts and connections in the industry, as well as a good reputation within it, is a good thing to do as soon as you can. This is an investment in terms of time and money on your part. But a good script consultant/editor will make sure you get value for money and, in this way, you will be improving your writing and chances of being seen and read by the industry.

The vast majority of writers are a pleasure to work with and we both benefit from the work we do together. I learn a lot by working with so many different personalities and on a varied and fascinating slate of projects. Conversely for the writer, I understand from the endorsements and kind comments I receive, that they feel they have benefited from my process of structure and development. However, working in this way with a script consultant or script editor can be both exposing and a bit scary at first for the writer. Being required to look at your project through the prism of someone else's eyes, even if that someone comes to the table with decades of experience in the field, is still daunting and not something every writer is ready to do. Change, as anyone trying to make differences in their lives will tell you, is hard. So before you decide to work with a professional, come out of your private writing state and enter a collaborative one. Make sure you are ready to take on the difference this working relationship will make to you, both as a writer, and to your project as a whole.

INTERVIEWS WITH
KEY INDUSTRY PLAYERS

Over Zoom, I had the pleasure of catching up with the varied, exciting, award-studded careers of some of my friends and colleagues in the industry. These are the writers who are creating some of your favourite dramas and the producers behind them. Everyone I picked out here for the book is passionate, driven and committed to the work they create. There are no easy ways in here. There's no sitting back and letting things slide – all of these people have worked their socks off to be where they are now. Amongst other things, we discussed drama development in general, what makes a good story for television tick and what makes a successful drama for television.

JAKE LUSHINGTON - HEAD OF DRAMA, WORLD PRODUCTIONS

Jake and I share mutual friends in common in real life and on social media. We both worked as script editors on *EastEnders* (not at the same time) and he also script edited one of my favourite shows ever, *This Life*, made by World Productions. Jake and his team at World Productions recently took home the International Emmy for the innovative, brave and unique series *Vigil*. He also produced *The Bletchley Circle* for ITV and, most recently, executive produced *Suspect*, again for ITV.

ON PITCHING

Yvonne: Do you get pitched at literally all the time?

Jake: Not verbally very much, normally it's by email. And then, if I'm interested, I might meet the person or have a further conversation.

Yvonne: Do you normally get a one-pager or a treatment to start the conversation?

Jake: It depends. It could be a full script. Most of what I read comes from agented writers but I do get recommendations from places like the National Television School and people like yourself.

ON PROJECTS

Jake: The key thing is, we always ask ourselves the same question: 'Do we think it's interesting and do we think we can sell it?' And actually there are things we can sell which we don't find interesting. And that's one, two, three years of my life, so I have to think about that very carefully as a producer. Just because it's got a clear commercial angle which means I can sell it, if I don't like it, that's not good enough. It's the same thing with the writer – this will be a person I'll be speaking to for two to three years – and for the director. These will be crucial relationships during the development, production and post-production of the show, so I need to feel I can work closely with these people.

ON TERRESTRIALS

Jake: Terrestrial channels no longer have the money – your average budget for a 9 o'clock drama has gone from £700,000-£900,000 in 2012 to £1.5 million-£1.9 million now, and that's still the cheaper end.

Yvonne: So terrestrials are struggling to produce the competing shows.

Jake: They are. And we are struggling. A lot of solid, competitive production companies are struggling these days. You have to know how expensive your show is from the get-go and balance the investment necessary with the payoff in terms of audience and financial recoup.

ON WRITERS' ROOMS

Yvonne: We haven't caught up with the Americans on this way of creating long runners.

Jake: There are far more writers' rooms now than a few years ago. The big Netflix shows – *Gangs of London* for example – are all team-written. The streamer culture has meant we are leaning more on the core series being created by a team in a writers' room than we did before.

Yvonne: Yes, I've noticed a more pronounced reliance on that way of working in recent years.

Jake: The real difference with Americans in terms of writing teams is they have money to put people in rooms for years. The proportion of the production budget that is spent on writers is 30 per cent to 35 per cent and here, in the UK, it is 10 per cent.

ON *VIGIL*

Jake: On the first series we had two other writers apart from Tom Edge (series creator) writing episodes. On series 2 we have a room with Tom Edge and three other writers. So only five in total. It's a tight and inclusive team.

Yvonne: As exec, do you run the writers' room? Or do you let them run it?

Jake: I'm not there regularly. I was in the room a lot in series 1 of *Vigil* – I have a background in soap storytelling – which you know!

Yvonne: Yes. We share a history of *EastEnders*!

Jake: But on series 2 I have been busy on a show in post-production so I drop into the story room but my head of development for Scotland, George (Aza-Selinger), runs the room. I'm coming in and giving notes, but I'm a bit further back on this series.

ON *THE SUSPECT*

Jake: *The Suspect* was a book in a series of nine books. I read it in 2014 and pitched for the rights then and I didn't get it. It went elsewhere and they developed it and couldn't get it away. At the end of 2018, early 2019, I was speaking to Val Hoskins (Jake's agent) who told me it was free again. I said: 'Well, was there a script?' It turned out they weren't happy enough to show it to anybody. So I said: 'In that case, I'm interested.' I think the fact that it went in with a dubious protagonist rather than the police as POV is more of a challenging watch. I think it's more of a thriller than a procedural and I liked that angle. The network said write a script and to be honest Peter (Berry) wrote a brilliant pilot – it's a real page-turner. So they said get the script right and it's a go. I think there's a lot of people who think you have to hustle for every commission – but I think the ones that happen will happen and those that don't – just don't.

Yvonne: That's a clear message for writers! A lot of people I work with get frustrated. I'm not known. I'm no good at networking. I don't feel confident to pitch well. But really, at the end of the day, if your script is strong and your story is marketable, that'll get you through the door, in the initial stages at least.

Jake: That's it. I've taken a chance on spec scripts that have got away and those that haven't. As long as they have a certain quality that I can get behind, and they can be read by broadcasters, we will see how far we can go.

ON AGENTS

Yvonne: What's your take on writer representation? Do they have to be represented to get in a room with you?

Jake: The being repped thing is hard. But I have got some people their first gigs and first commissions – it's not entirely unheard of. More worrying for me is if they won't collaborate. It's a collaborative process. And for me that's true if it's Jed Mercurio or some unknown writer. What's your working relationship like? If it's good, you will make a better show.

ON STORYTELLING

Jake: Anything that depends on some reversal to engage the audience is not good storytelling. There is a presumption that the audience always loves to not know things. It's not true.

ON JED MERCURIO

Yvonne: What's it like working with someone who is as confident and strong a storyteller as Jed (Mercurio)?

Jake: I worked with him as a producer (*Line of Duty*/created and written by Jed Mercurio/World Productions). I think the great thing about that is that you are working with someone who already has great story ideas, so what you are doing in the development process is getting a VIP pass to a much more interactive world where you can come in and go 'oh what about this' and it's accepted and batted about. There's a self-assurance to that, which comes with experience.

The other thing I always like to share about Jed is that he will get to episode 3 and decide he wants to kill x and then you say, 'But episode 1 and 2 have nothing to do with that set-up', and he says 'Yeah, I know I'll have to go back and rewrite episode 1 and 2.' What Jed always talks about is 'fulfilling the dull creative arc'. You go, 'Oh yes, we start here, we reach this bit and we end here,' and the trouble with that (which Jed hates) is that you already know what is going to happen and, for a writer, in his book, that's fatal. He says, 'I trust myself that by the end there'll be a good character arc, and if that's not the case, I'll rewrite it till there is.' I'd rather be in that position, as a producer. For a writer with the confidence of Jed, for instance, whereby I am like an audience member, watching this thing sequentially.

That feeling of not knowing where it's going to end up. You can smell that in the writing.

TONY JORDAN – WRITER/PRODUCER AND FOUNDER/ CEO OF RED PLANET PRODUCTIONS

Tony was one of the first writers I ever script edited on *EastEnders* in 1990/1991 when Tony was (arguably) the king of that soap. The year I worked on the show, he created the ratings-busting scenario for the Mitchell brothers (characters created by Tony in 1990) when Grant was in prison for GBH, giving Phil, his brother, often considered weaker, the chance to go under the radar and conduct an affair with Sharon, Grant's wife. We storylined the scenario to span a year's episodes and at the end of the year I worked on the show, 22 million people watched the episode where Grant discovers his brother's and wife's betrayal. Tony is one of the key writers behind the hugely successful *Life on Mars* (Kudos/BBC Wales) which he created and co-wrote with Ashley Pharoah and Matthew Graham. Tony also created and wrote *Hustle* for Kudos Film and Television/ BBC 1. Tony's company Red Planet Productions is the powerhouse behind many ratings big-hitters, including *Death in Paradise*, created by Robert Thorogood.

ON CREATIVE VS COMMERCIAL

Tony: The worst thing any writer can say to me is 'I've found a gap in the market.' The industry is split into two very different parts – creative and corporate. They both have to balance each other. There is zero corporate without creative because there is nothing to sell. There is an element of creative without corporate but as creatives we will all starve. They have to co-exist. A rule from my perspective – a rule at Red Planet, and a rule throughout development – is you must not start the process in the wrong Venn diagram. Don't start the creative process in the corporate world. And don't use the creative thing in the corporate world. You will go bankrupt.

Yvonne: What makes the person with the money invest in the show?

Tony: Like everything in the world, there is an ideal and there's the reality. The ideal is you write a script with a cracking story and it is an irresistible idea. Someone at one of the networks reads it, thinks it's brilliant and says let's make it. But the reality is a lot of execs at networks commission on fear. They can get the best script in the world but if it's not written by an A-lister that they know, they won't want to commission it. They will commission a shit script because they've got a great talent – a director or an actor – attached. That's why you see shit on television and shit in the movies. It made corporate sense to take the risk. There's so much money in the industry it can't be just a creative industry.

ON PLANNING AND STRUCTURE

Yvonne: I always get warning flags when writers say, 'It's my characters, they tell me what to do.' I say, 'Stop that, you need an outline. You need to build into peaks to know where you are going with it. Plan ahead where the end of your story arc is. You need to know the beginning, the middle and the end before you commit to that script.' Would you agree with that?

Tony: Some. I think you need... how the fuck do I know what *you* need? I know what *I* need... I need to know what my first image is. When the show starts. I also need to know the end image. The middle will take care of itself along the way. Has to be said, I hate any kind of outline or treatment. I hate it.

ON PITCHING

Tony: You need to say as little as you can for the person you are pitching to, to be dying to ask, 'What happens next?'

ON BEING A WRITER

Tony: People often ask me how they can become a writer. Who's stopping you from being a writer? Who are they? Who do I need to talk to on your behalf? Who's fucking stopping you writing? Because I'm going to get those bastards. What are they doing? Have they nicked your pens? Have they nicked your paper? These people are not asking how to be a writer – they are asking how am I going to get paid to be a writer? Who the fuck knows? I say just do it and keep doing it.

If you call yourself a writer, then just write. Write like nobody is ever going to read it. Write with a little bit of integrity, a little bit of passion and write a cracking story with cracking characters. And work fucking hard. Once you've written it, rewrite it and rewrite it – 50 times. Then show it to somebody and, if you're talented, you will become a success.

And if you can't write, then people won't buy it so just do it as a hobby. But never ever say to me you want to be a writer because, if you've got a WH Smith near you, nothing is stopping you.

SARAH CONROY – EXECUTIVE PRODUCER, FURTHER SOUTH PRODUCTIONS

Sarah and I were both at Granada TV at the same time and became friends there. Later, she was a vital and integral member of my script team on *Crossroads*. Sarah went on to become Commissioning Editor for Drama at ITV and, most recently, Executive Producer at Lionsgate TV and Further South Productions.

ON WORKING WITH AUTHORS TRANSITIONING TO TELEVISION

We would never want to shape a writer's experience or speak for them. Their experience is what makes their story authentic. But when new to screenwriting, that writer might need help with, say, the structural side of how to tell their story on screen. So as producers we would try to help them with structure, whilst staying true to their vision and the essence of their work. We would also help them work out the mechanics of the story in terms of what would work best for TV. Hopefully, we enable the writer to still bring their own voice and experience to the screen from the novel.

ON WRITERS

Yvonne: It was an unwritten thing that as a writer you needed to earn your stripes. Do a couple of soaps, get a couple of *Casualties* and then the industry would take you seriously. I see this has changed over recent years and now the onus is on your personal voice as a writer.

Sarah: I think that first person, authentic experience, is something we have become more drawn to over the years in TV.

Yvonne: Would you consider a new writer? Or do you go to agents that you like for the new ideas?

Sarah: We would always consider new writers to TV. When I say new, however, they would have usually had some experience writing in the dramatic form whether that be through novel-writing or theatre. In terms of ideas, some come from agents, some from existing relationships with writers and a lot of material we started out with came from books. The fact that there is an Intellectual Property already and it's going to bring in an audience – it seems to be important to everyone at the moment.

Yvonne: I say that if you have worked solo on your writer voice for over a year, you will gain more from working with me than if you are a totally new writer. If you are too green, you won't understand what I am trying to do with your work and I won't feel I am helping you and we'll both be crying!

Sarah: This can happen. Sometimes you can assume new writers know what you're talking about but, because they don't want to question the process and risk looking naive, they perhaps don't feel able to ask. It's always best to be honest at the outset when you're developing a project. You both have to feel passionate about the process but trust the other person enough to ask the questions.

LISA HOLDSWORTH – WRITER

Lisa is one of the industry's genuinely good gals. She's a focused, funny writer with a big heart to match. Lisa's writing credits are wide and varied. She has written an impressive amount of serialised, popular drama for all the major channels. From *Emmerdale, Fat Friends, New Tricks, Waterloo Road, Midsomer Murders, Call The Midwife* and, most recently, *Dance School* for C4 which she co-created with Theresa Ikoko and is executive producer on the show. She has an infectious passion for the industry and is a vocal and strong supporter of new writers and the rights of all writers in the industry. She is chair of the Writers' Guild of Great Britain.

ON WORKING WITH ANOTHER WRITER ON A PROJECT

Yvonne: What was it like working with Theresa on *Dance School*? How did it differ from the solo development you do?

Lisa: It was a very different experience working with another writer on a development project. Usually, you're bouncing the ideas off a development exec who will guide but not really throw in their own ideas. With another writer there can be too many ideas! Conflicts have to be dealt with carefully so no one dominates or is made to feel like the 'junior partner'. Luckily both Theresa and I are pretty robust in the way we fight our corners and we had lots of common ground. Still, it was useful to work with someone who was often coming from a different place in terms of culture and experience. And I think we ended up with something greater than the sum of its parts.

ON PITCHING

Yvonne: How did you go about creating the pitch and actually doing it? A lot of my writers need help in this area!

Lisa: The pitch was very much about selling the sizzle not the steak. We used lots of emotive language about how we wanted the audience to feel and what the experience of watching the show would be like. We also talked about our characters a huge amount and did some fantasy casting so commissioners had a good idea of who they were. It's a precinct drama and a gang show, so it was important to sell the world and those who populate it. Indeed, we kept the story content light so that we would have some surprises up our sleeves when it was commissioned.

ON BEING A SHOWRUNNER

We basically invited five writers into the room and pitched the show to them. Then we opened the floor to ideas, thoughts and even criticisms. The first week was very free-flowing with lots of discussions about character and what might drive them. By the time we came to the second week we were in love with our characters and – in that sadistic way writers do – set about making their lives hell! Again we talked very emotionally about what we wanted to feel as the stories unfolded. We wanted pain but also joy, loss but also triumph. We also sought to subvert some of the clichés of dance movies. Then Theresa and I went away and worked up a series outline document.

ON WORKING ON AN ESTABLISHED SHOW

Yvonne: You are known for writing some of the most popular shows on TV. What's the process like working on *Midsomer Murders* or *Call the Midwife*?

Lisa: There is still a degree of pitching when it comes to shows like that. *Midsomer Murders* particularly. You usually have to pitch ideas for the investigation part of the story and create the guest characters. So it is still a very creative process. Obviously, you have to be aware of the tone of the show and the regular characters and respect what has gone before.

On a lot of the regular shows, the showrunner/creator has moved on to new pastures, so you are usually dealing with executive producers. They keep a weather eye on the creative process but don't usually contribute. They know what they want and it's your job to provide it! Once the scriptwriting is underway, you tend to work directly with the script editor who will pass on notes from the exec, directors and (God help us) actors.

The exception to that is *Call the Midwife*. Heidi Thomas (creator/showrunner) is still very much hands on. Indeed, she storylines every episode and then asks you to expand on what she has written. She knows her show inside out and across all the extensive research whilst writing her own episodes. She has an extraordinary work ethic! Still, her notes do come via the script editors and producer.

ASHLEY PHAROAH – WRITER

Writer and co-creator of *Life on Mars*, creator and writer of *The Living and the Dead* and head writer of *Around the World in 80 Days*, Ashley's strong, visual, character-driven writing has been on our screens for the best part of 30 years. We started working together, me as a baby script editor, he as a new writer, on *EastEnders* in the early 1990s. He is a huge supporter of new work, and is passionate about the industry and his part in it.

ON THE DEVELOPMENT JOURNEY OF
THE LIVING AND THE DEAD

Monastic Productions (the company he set up with writer Matthew Graham) teamed up with Lookout to make my passion project, *The Living and the Dead*. Faith Penhale (Executive Producer, BBC Wales) started the ball rolling. We were talking about new projects and she said, 'What about a Victorian ghost story?' I had images of Victorian London and swirling fog, Jack the Ripper... you know...

On the train home back to Bath I thought, 'What if you set a ghost story in the countryside? What if you set it in the summer, largely in daytime and you set it at that time in history when the Industrial Revolution had just begun and was destroying the way of life that had been around for centuries?' If there was ever going to be unrest that's when it would be. Even as a kid I was a massive Thomas Hardy fan. I loved the strong complex women characters he had. By the time I got to Bath I thought, 'Fuck, I really want to write that.' I really love the ghost story genre and I could write about an area I come from.

Yvonne: So did you write a treatment first?

Ashley: I think I wrote a treatment. And episode 1 which fortunately went down really well. But they wanted an episode 2 because they wanted to know more about where it was going and what the format structure was. Then it was greenlit!

Yvonne: That's unusual.

Ashley: It was unusual. But we felt two episodes were needed just to make sure – gothic horror is an unusual genre for television. Matthew (Graham) and I pitched a six-part series – we storylined it together – and this was what was greenlit.

ON CHANGES IN THE DEVELOPMENT PROCESS

Then it came from somewhere – I've never found out where – but we heard back that they wanted it to be a 'story of the week' format. I had written about a third of the series at this point. We were also half way through storylining the whole thing. This threw us off kilter for a bit. It was bloody. The series, to us, felt completely different. And it wasn't what I set out to write. There was a fight with the broadcaster (BBC1) from the beginning to end.

ON EXECUTIVE PRODUCING

Yvonne: Sometimes the executive can get in the way... I found it frustrating when I was producing *Crossroads* because I wanted a more creative role and in the end, if you get to the point of executive producing, you sort of miss out on that level and it's all about putting out fires and managing people.

Ashley: I can see why writers want to showrun – you get a lot of creative clout and producers talk a lot about needing a showrunner these days but I don't think they need that – they need a lead writer who can also executive produce. The term showrunner has come from America but not the practice.

ON CREATIVE RELATIONSHIPS

Yvonne: Faith (Penhale) knew you well – she knew what makes you want to write. It started from a creative spark, and she and you had an understanding. She nurtured your writing talent. A lot of what I talk about with my writers is about forging those creative partnerships that ultimately benefit both of you.

Ashley: Yes, those relationships are incredibly important. You might have a drink at someone's leaving do and, as you well know, something might start from there. You just have to make sure when you start, you're a decent human being. Polite and kind to people going up and down!

Yvonne: So important not to be an arse!

ON GETTING INTO THE INDUSTRY

Ashley: When I see new writers moaning about trying to get into the industry, I have a lot of sympathy for them. Because I can go to a meeting and we will spend 10 minutes talking about the kids and 'do you remember that thing that happened 20 years ago?' You know? I can see, when I was on the outside looking in, I felt, 'God, they all know each other!' And there is a tiny bit of truth in that. I do think you give work to people you trust.

Yvonne: Creativity is what producers want, but they also want a safe, commercial bet – it's a hard thing to get right for a new writer for sure. And if you're not yet known, then it's hard to get across the line.

Ashley: Yes, but you also see writers' names now on some really big shows and you think, 'Who the fuck is that?' In a sense I feel like an old-fashioned rock band – you do the university circuit, then town halls and, if you're lucky, you end up at Wembley. I don't think that's the trajectory any more. I don't think they do three years on *EastEnders* and maybe two on *Casualty*. I've worked with writers and it can be their first or second gig on an established show and you ask if they want to come back for a second series and they're like, 'I want to do my own stuff now.' And sometimes – they do!

ON SERIES DISCIPLINE

Yvonne: In the main, new writers are not strong on long-running series narratives – how to control that.

Ashley: That's true, that's why people like me will always do OK now. Because growing up in that system, that's what me and you did. We planted things in the storyline and we knew we had to expand on them and pay them off.

STEVE MATTHEWS – EXECUTIVE PRODUCER FOR BANIJAY – NORDIC COUNTRIES AND SPAIN

Steve Matthews was my story lifeline back in 2002. I was anxiously trying to crew up the last metamorphosis of *Crossroads* and finding it hard to hire story people with the right mix of experience in handling writers and the long-form narrative, as well as a genuine love of the job. I needed a team player with tons of story kudos who was also a leader and an innovator. Steve Matthews was my story producer for *Crossroads* and oversaw the storylines and script editors.

Yvonne: Your remit was working with writers across the board in Central Europe for HBO and now, for Banijay, developing the work of writers for Nordic Countries and Spain. This means that you are familiar with working in a room of writers, with writing teams, with writer duos – all the configurations basically...

Steve: Yes, and my job is essentially to supply great drama content, by developing new talent in those regions. For HBO there was only one buyer above Antony Root but for Banijay there are several buyers for different production companies but essentially it's the same thing. When I started at HBO and was focused on Central Europe the job was all about me going to Hungary and supporting the Hungarian teams to do Hungarian projects, with Hungarian writers back in 2014, but with the rise of the streamer market things have changed somewhat since then.

Yvonne: Now, more than ever, I feel we need writers who understand how to develop and handle series narrative, to create strong stories.

Steve: Exactly, the training is really important. I have always formed a bridge between the training and the development of a project. One side there's the money and, on the other, there's the creative, developmental side.

Yvonne: Yes, so the questions we ask are: what makes a project commercial, what's the engagement factor and what is attracting an audience? What's the angle that makes an audience want to watch?

Steve: What I increasingly say to my writers is stuff has to happen. Protagonist, goal, quest, barrier, Antagonist, reversal, payoff. You need to see and feel those peaks in the narrative.

Yvonne: Exactly. The series structure is all about avoiding the flatline of a narrative.

Steve: What a series really is, to my mind, is a series of arcs.

Yvonne: Gosh, so important. I work with arcs all the time.

Steve: You think like I do. We grew up in television from the soap and series background, talking about this stuff.

Yvonne: Now streamers really need this knowledge to be behind the stories they invest in.

Steve: A series is not one single arc, like the structure of a feature. A TV series has an additional series of arcs, each episode in effect, forming that overarching structure so every episode has its own engine. You have to find the internal dynamic that keeps it going. Family is the key structure for a TV series I find. It may be a metaphorical precinct family like *Downton Abbey* or the hospital backdrop like in *Grey's Anatomy*, or a real, if dysfunctional one, like in *The Sopranos* or *Succession*.

Yvonne: The ensemble effect of a series based on a family, be it a sitcom situation like *The Royle Family* or the tight-knit friend grouping of *It's A Sin,* is definitely a strong series structure and one tailor-made for streamers.

Steve: The world of the streamer has changed the face of television. Whether it be a high-concept piece or something contemporary and character-driven like *Fleabag,* where characters are floating around having thematic conversations, that first 30 seconds is so important. There's so much content out there now. A project that is just OK is not going to get through. I tell my Central European writers – don't be boring. Tell a story and make it interesting.

Yvonne: I believe that characters create plot. Textually the subtext drives it.

Steve: Yes, I believe Jonathon Young said 'audience comes for the story but comes back for the characters'. And this is another big difference between film and television. It is all about character. The really magical characters don't just have a want – you know – a Robert McKee want/ need line. The compelling characters like Walter White and Tony Soprano are the ones that time and time again shift, change, they keep growing, they keep developing. Sometimes we feel they are really bad and then we think 'oh, I understand how they feel, I get that.'

Yvonne: So we are watching the evolution of a character rather than the prescribed arc for them?

Steve: Yes and we are pushing writers to be more plot-driven. The gold standard is something like *The Undoing*... the central character is good, no, he's bad, no, he's good again – we engage with him/them because of our emotional investment.

Yvonne: Does genre play a big part in your development work with writers?

Steve: Right, so of course the genre will have a big impact on the story you want to tell, and like I said earlier, stuff has to happen – there has to be plot – but none of these things means anything if the series doesn't have a heart. We have got to have some reason to watch it. I tell my writers all the time: genre and art are not two separate things. Don't look down on genre. It doesn't reduce the characters. Think of it more like a lens through which we could heighten the story and the characters.

Yvonne: Yes, interesting, so we have the driver/plot aesthetic and the character coming from within... that's the sweet spot to achieve. I felt that *Succession* did that well although there's an element of cypher to the characters.

Steve: And it was a good time to be considering billionaires, money, the media – that show hit the zeitgeist which is always a great thing to happen. There's a piece of magic when you're constructing a television series, like with any type of art, there's an element you can't control. You certainly can't plan the zeitgeist. You have to be behind the curve to make it work, but if you do tap into what's going on now then that's the luck and the magic working. I often say to writers, look there's two parts of writing – particularly television writing. There is the left brain part of it: the meetings, the office white board, the planning, the A, B, C stories – the geometry of it – and then there's the magic part. That's when you are wide awake at 3am in the morning waiting for the story to come.

Yvonne: Yes, waiting for inspiration to hit so the rest of it can follow. That combination of creativity and planning – it's a wonderful thing when it works!

Steve: And essentially, a buyer, a producer, a broadcaster, are all going to be focusing on the same area – the core idea. So I always say to writers bringing their ideas to me, there are three questions to answer. Why have you brought this to us to make? Why are you the writer to deliver this project? And finally, and crucially, one writers often find hardest to answer, why now? Why make this show now? Why today and not last year?

Yvonne: Do you think writers have to write what they know?

Steve: That's a good question – do you need to know personally the world of your story? I don't think you do. But you need to know your world. There is something to be said for an idea that has a really strong personal resonance with a writer.

Yvonne: But obviously that's not a recipe that can be delivered all the time.

Steve: Exactly, but certainly the idea has to feel totally rooted, totally credible and somehow the heart has to come out of it.

Yvonne: Having a personal connection to a story can do that or if you immerse yourself in character and research the world you are in.

Steve: So the emotional grounding is totally solid. I say to writers, if you want to get three or four years out of this idea, you need to know this world right down to its soul – because if you don't then you may lose sight of that little magic light in the dark; when the notes system kicks in and everyone's got an opinion, then you really need to know your world. It's the series like *Shameless* that resonate strongly. Paul Abbott knew exactly what he was doing – he knew exactly what it was, right into its soul.

SARAH PINBOROUGH – NOVELIST/SCREENWRITER

Social media can work for you in a good way, writers. I met Sarah via mutual friends on Facebook. It was Ted, her fabulously charismatic dog/boy, that I think we first communicated about. Thanks Ted for the introduction! Sarah is currently working on several original screen projects and adaptations with producers in the UK and across the pond. Her fabulously intriguing and multi-layered thriller novel *Behind Her Eyes* was adapted for television by Steven Lightfoot and *The Crown* producers, Left Bank Productions. It made a huge impact on our sensibilities in

2021 via Netflix and earned a trending hashtag #thatending on Twitter.

ON THE DEVELOPMENT OF BEHIND HER EYES FOR TELEVISION

Sarah: I remember going in to the meeting with Left Bank and I had just been in LA and had done literally dozens of meetings about this book and I just didn't want to sell it to TV. Netflix were only just coming in and TV was seen as secondary – everyone I had met up to that point was talking about film. But when I went into Left Bank, the whole team was at the table. Andy Harries (CEO/founder of Left Bank) and Jess (Jessica Burdett, executive producer) were big champions of it. I came out of there and I was like, 'Yeah, I want to sell it to them, they'll get it made.' And they absolutely did and it was so fast! They tried to sell it to the BBC who wanted to change the ending because that's what the BBC always want to do. Netflix in America were reading it at the same time. Left Bank and Netflix made *The Crown* together. Soon Steve (Lightfoot) was on board to write it, and they greenlit it without seeing a script. They really, really wanted to make it and trusted Steve to write it well and there was a trust between Netflix and Left Bank.

ON THE WRITING OF THE TV ADAPTATION

Sarah: My agent said, 'Don't you want to write it?' and I said, 'No! I've spent two years writing the book, publicising it, talking about it to everyone – I just want to get it made!' Steve did such a good job of it. What he doesn't get enough credit for is that it is a very internalised book and he took a lot of the internal monologue and externalised it into action without veering from the original storyline.

Yvonne: When you're around TV people it's always to do with the angle, the engagement factor, it's that development journey that you have to go on with your story – building along that arc across an elongated length of time. Not all novelists can do that easily.

Sarah: I'm not a great fan of adapting my own novels – I find that boring. Now I have a manager and agent and they all want you to adapt your own stuff because it's easy money. I have been sent so many books which I haven't adapted because there's no fucking story. And in my experience, no one reads the book! Maybe they do in the UK, but in Hollywood, no one talking to you about the adaptation has read the book. They want you to pitch the whole story – the beginning, the middle and the end – and then if you go further down the line, it's up to you and whoever else is on the writing team to beat out the rest of it. The studios pile in and get the rights and then it's up to the writers to do the rest. Everyone wants something that's based on something already. They like the blurb – the shiny parts – which you have to pull out to sell for them.

CHRIS LUNT AND MIKE WALKER, WRITING TEAM

I connected with Chris via LinkedIn and Facebook (use social media to make these healthy connections for yourselves, writers!). Chris is a writing workhorse. His work ethic is second to none. He has a naturally commercial mindset and loves to create strong muscular story engines that drive all the work he makes. His big break into the industry came via his series *Prey* (Red Productions/ITV), and he and his writing partner Mike Walker have since worked on many long runners in the UK and abroad including *Devils* (Sky Atlantic), *Young Wallander* (Yellow Bird/Netflix) and *The Swarm* (Schwarm TV Productions).

ON CHRIS'S START AS A WRITER

Chris: I got some redundancy money from the job I had left and my wife said you can have a crack at becoming a professional writer but once that money has gone, you're going to have to get another job. So I got two projects to script stage. One was called *Masks* and the other was *Prey*. *Masks* did really well at first but fell at a late stage with the BBC. I knew Steve November who was producing *Emmerdale* at the time. I went to meet him but, by the time I got there, I knew I didn't want to write for the show so I came clean and we talked about other projects. We got on well and I knew his wife Hayley. Steve was about to move on so it was good timing.

ON THE DEVELOPMENT OF *PREY*

Chris: When Steve moved from *Emmerdale* to commission series for ITV he asked me in again to talk about my projects. I told him about *Masks* and *Prey*. Which one did I prefer, he wanted to know. I felt *Prey* was more commercial so I put that forward. He made me write two episodes to make sure I had the tone and the format nailed and then he greenlit it.

ON WORKING TOGETHER

Chris: Mike and I were introduced to each other by Jed Mercurio, who was signed up to do a sci-fi series that unfortunately never took off. Mike and I were in a room with three or four writers and a producer. We just gelled and we had similar personalities and work ethics, and coincidentally, were represented by the same agency, Casarotto. After that, we seemed to be continually put up for the same jobs. As a consequence of us being in that first interview we became mates and, after a round of seeing each other at the same gigs for writing, we thought why not team up and then we'd have a better chance of landing the same gig. *Devils* started soon after we made this decision and we were parachuted in as showrunners. Also, during that time, we got really close to writing on the second series of *The Night Manager* but we wouldn't have been lead writers and we didn't like being second or third fiddle in the writing room. Then I had a meeting with Frank Doelger (showrunner on *Game of Thrones*). He was doing a big international co-production ecological/thriller series called *The Swarm*. I had to go down to London and, in a heartbeat, I was going to cancel it because I felt we ought to take *The Night Manager*. I thought it was a general meet but Frank said, 'I want you to have a crack at it.' I told him I had a writing partner and so I called Mike and said, 'We'll be in charge of this one.' And so we took it.

ON WORKING IN A WRITERS' ROOM

Mike: Sometimes when you're working with a producer in a room with other writers, it goes around in circles. You start talking the minutiae and get too into details. Chris and I are used to getting down the bare bones, the basic framework of the story first. Then we break it down further, we write it up and we swap events and sequences around. The initial breakdown is very quick and then we spend a few days getting the outline down. That's when we go into detail to see what is working and what isn't.

ON WHAT MAKES A GOOD SCRIPT

Chris: Make sure people want to read the second script by writing all the seeds and hooks in the first. They must feel like they've 'seen' the episode they've just read. It's got to be entirely visually clear and smooth. Don't interrupt it with camera talk. Mike on occasion writes, 'We see x going into the building', for instance. I always take them out!

Mike: I still like a 'we see'.

Yvonne: Me too.

Chris: But you must pull the reader in. Make them forget they're reading. You only have one chance to get the script sold – it's all down to that script.

JAN MCVERRY – WRITER

Jan very deservedly won the Tony Warren Award recently for outstanding contribution to the television landscape and has, since the mid-1990s, been a core member on the writing team of *Coronation Street,* the soap Tony created back in 1961. We met at Granada Television in the 1990s and she shared similar experiences working as both a script editor, storyliner and then full-time writer for the drama series department. Jan has literally been there and bought the tee shirt. What she doesn't know about writing the long-form narrative is not worth knowing.

ON STORYTELLING IN GENERAL

Yvonne: I do think, being at Granada during those years (the 1990s), working directly with, or breathing the same air as, Paul Abbott, Kay Mellor and Peter Whalley, we picked up an ethos around story that wasn't ever officially 'taught'.

Jan: I get asked a lot about how to tell stories for TV and I always feel it's a bit of a low-rent answer but true, when I say a lot of how I approach story is done by instinct.

Yvonne: Totally.

Jan: I wonder if the way we learned to use the act structure was because we were crafting story for a commercial channel. So we had to address the ad breaks – literally – the thing that would break the story for us. So we had to build whatever was happening to encompass that enforced break in the narrative.

Yvonne: I love that. It's so true. It's affected how I think about story for myself, but also for the writers I work with, ever since really.

Jan: I am from a storylining background – I need to know where I'm going in a story. I need to produce a document that sells the story. So the creative mindset is tied into the commercial all the time. Your drive is to put down a basic story arc and go from there.

Yvonne: And there's that tricky thing where you realise that what you have isn't actually a story.

Jan: Yeah, that's when you realise it's a situation – a series of isolated moments.

Yvonne: And then you have to go back to the character.

Jan: When I worked on *Brookside*, Phil (Redmond creator/ executive producer) was all about the issues of the day really, more of a social realist than anything. When I joined GTV I learned early on that to apply the issue on top – literally this is the plot – doesn't work. The issue has to come from character – filtered through their lens so it doesn't creak and is totally authentic. So it doesn't – to use a Russell T (Davies) word – become 'worthy'.

ON PITCHING

Yvonne: You obviously pitch story all the time at *Coronation Street* story conference. How does this differ for you when you are pitching a story, to another outfit, that's your original creation?

Jan: Definitely scarier! It's more exposing because at *Corrie*, you have the support of the show essentially behind you there. It's all about plot isn't it? Producers want to know where it's going. What happens next.

Yvonne: And the hardest question to answer sometimes... what's this about?

Jan: God, yeah.

Yvonne: And I used to feel, pitching to the ITV Network when I was at GTV, I had to fill the silences – fill the gaps – you know, with talking.

Jan: God, I had to do that too and it's very hard, isn't it? But you need to do your prep. Even if you haven't worked the whole thing out, you need to have a clear idea of where the story is moving across that basic arc and who the main characters are.

ON WRITING FOR *CORONATION STREET*

Jan: It used to be that you could come to story conference and not have a story to pitch – it was in the contract but it wasn't generally thought that you *had* to do a pitch. But now, it's different – you do need to supply the show with the material it needs. But there's a lovely support there. I've worked on shows where you're feeling, 'If I don't get this story across, I'll lose my job.' But that's not the case on *Corrie*.

Yvonne: I think as a producer, it depends on the show you are making, but certainly for me, I have found that I had to have the security of a strong story team behind me to generate those storylines that we then expected the writers to flesh out. It's a budget thing more than anything when you take that approach.

Jan: Absolutely – it depends on the show of course. But *Corrie* is writer-led and we are a robust team. We know how to get our voices across and at story conference – even the short terms – you need to come prepared to pitch story and to give the broad arc of it. We are actually friends as a team – we don't constantly go out with each other or whatever, but we do have each other's backs. And newer writers to the team are welcomed with a kindness.

ON CREATING A HIT STORYLINE

Jan: I had this storyline about domestic violence – the victim being a male. The producer at the time, Phil Collinson, didn't believe it and we couldn't find the right fix for the character, so although it was there, in the back of my mind, I had to get the time right to pitch it. Finally we got it away really well for Tyrone Dobbs, and that was so great because I felt it landed properly there. We weren't preaching. It felt right – this was an angle that worked because he's such a lovely character.

ON THE WRITER MINDSET

Yvonne: And on a long runner often there's a regular changeover of producers – the script team may find themselves suffering under this 'new broom' mindset some producers employ. How do you cope with that?

Jan: I learned early on not to take anything personally. So sometimes a producer might not like my writing as much as, say, the previous one did. But you just keep digging in and staying true to your voice. All we have as writers is our confidence. And the writing team on *Corrie* knows that. You stay true to the show, try and deliver the tone and stories the producer wants and, if it's really tough, you stay the course – there'll be another one along at some point! I say Evolution rather than Revolution!

Yvonne: I love that! We need that on a tea towel...

JEREMY DRYSDALE - WRITER

I met Jeremy through the powerful attraction of Facebook algorithms. He is a delightful, funny, crazily clever, acerbic writer who writes with passionate focus. This writer knows what he wants to write and why. He is very direct and dynamic in both his writing and his approach to writing. Jeremy wrote the global bestselling single player game *Battlefield 2* and most recently the American action thriller feature *(In The) Line of Duty*. He understands how to hold a room and have his voice heard.

ON WRITING GENERALLY

Jeremy: Very good writers are being stolen from our screens because they're paid vastly more by Americans or streamers. I know Brit writers who write a show, it goes pretty well, and they go to America and you never see them again. Twenty years ago I wrote a sitcom – the only time I've ever written comedy. It was set in a hospital for the criminally insane. I've never done things the way you're supposed to do them, and this time was no exception although I didn't know any better at the time. I wrote six episodes and took it to a producer, and he was shocked. Producers, I learned then, don't want to read all that stuff.

Yvonne: When you're pitching to a producer you're trying to be both as succinct and as interesting as you can be at the same time. That's why I push my writers to write treatments that break their shows down into bite-sized chunks – you know – for a producer to digest easily. You have to stick to a certain format here essentially – I imagine you hate that?

Jeremy: I do hate it. I rarely verbally pitch to anyone these days. I was talking to someone at Channel 4 recently, and they said, 'If you are going to pitch something to us now, it has to have a social realism message.' Honestly, Yvonne, I couldn't give two shits about a social realistic message. I'm not interested.

ON AMERICA VS BRITAIN

If I'm writing an American thing they look at me and say, 'He may not have written for TV before but he's written multimillion-dollar movies and the best video game in history. So we know he can write.' The writer of *The Queen's Gambit* had never written for television before. The writer of *Mare of Easttown* did not have television experience but they still commissioned it. Over here, my understanding is that they don't like commissioning writers for TV who don't have a significant track record. I hear you are expected to go through the popular series like *Doctors* and work your way up. Well, I mean – fuck that.

ON TALKING WITH TARANTINO

I wanted to ask him about writing movies. He said, 'I write my scripts by hand. I can't spell properly. I haven't got time to format. I write as much dialogue as I want to. I have no interest at all in structure or act breaks etc. I just write the thing and give it to people and if they don't want it that's fine.'

ON FILM VS TELEVISION

Jeremy: I take things I've learnt in film and transfer them to TV because I don't see any difference in them. There's difference in length but that's it really. The only difference I can see is that TV needs a hook. You're going to disagree with me.

Yvonne: Yes, I do. For me, TV and film are different languages.

Jeremy: Really? I completely disagree with that.

Yvonne: Have you ever written in a room with other writers?

Jeremy: No, I don't like other writers.

OUTRO – SELF CONFIDENCE

Like it or not, we are writers, and specifically writers who want to get our stories out to the world of television – writing for the story-hungry, market-led world of commissioners, producers, streamers and broadcasters. We have to be savvy with our stories. They have to have emotional impact, strong story engines, a marketable angle and a focused net large enough to catch a loyal audience.

Confidence is everything. But it is often lacking as we present ourselves every day to the balefully blinking laptop screen. Do what you can to harness your inner critic and get your work out there. Then you can fake it until you make it with the people who can potentially make your stories real. Remember, they are fighting their own inner critics too so you're in good company. My inner critic's voice sounds like Jane Horrocks. She was there, haranguing me throughout the writing of my first commissioned script and latterly, for some unfathomable reason, Benedict Cumberbatch is sniffing pithily as I write my series outline of an idea I am currently working on. Writers are their own worst enemy.

As a producer and an executive producer, making shows like *Holby City* and *Crossroads,* I had to put my confidence in my script team and it was well placed. Good producers surround themselves with the best people who love their job and then they let them do that job. I had my job to do. I needed to give the overview of the show as a whole; to see the bigger picture and to address the stories from the story conference to the camera ready scripts with an eye that tied in the tone and the look of the show that the network had commissioned me to make.

My amazing script team were responsible for the detail and to make sure my notes were addressed in the time frame we had. They sat between me and the writing team. I know, because I was a script editor for a long time too, that this place can be quite uncomfortable to manage at times. But the business of drama production waits for no one and there's no time when you are on a show to doubt yourself or your ability to do your job. As a producer – effectively a manager of product and people – you must show your confidence even if you don't always feel it.

Producing is hard – there are stresses and pressures on your shoulders no other person in the huge drama factory that is any given series production studio has to carry. But here's the rub – I believe being a writer in that environment is just as hard. And self-confidence again is key here.

Embrace the Janes and Benedicts in your psyche – they can help if you listen correctly. The creative process is never straightforward and without that voice saying, 'Is this really interesting? Is this engaging? Do you know what you are doing here? Why should anyone care about this story, these characters?' as you are writing, perhaps you would never make your script any better. It is through the process of facing up to the doubter in you that you will create a piece of writing that you truly believe in. And then... well, a lovely thing happens. You have got your self-confidence back.

IN SUMMARY...

Use the process I outlined in this book to help you firstly get your idea on paper and build a structure around it. Get your treatment and your series outline written. Then make your pilot as good as it can be to sell the rest of your series. Get help from a professional script editor/consultant that you trust, that you know has done the work themselves and has a track record that you can check up on with writers and producers. Then let them help you raise your writing bar and hone your project for market with you.

Obviously, if you have an agent let them do their best work but, if not, then make strides towards getting yourself represented after you have at least three strong projects under your belt that you are proud of. There's a chapter in my book, *Writing for Television: Series, Serials and Soaps,* that deals with agents and how to get a good one.

Invest in yourself financially and creatively. Each day write something towards the completion of your TV project. Keep a diary or journal about your process and your achievements.

Read a lot of television scripts. Watch a lot of television series. Analyse why you like/dislike a certain series. Use the red line that edges its way along the bottom of your screen as you watch streamers. Stop that line at the tenth minute. There'll be something good happening at this point. This is because it is the end of Act 1 and, in a 5-act structure in an hour's drama, this often lands on page 10. Do the same geeky line stop at the midpoint of the episode. Again, something interesting should be happening there. Consider how the acts build in this episode to the end point. Use this in your own work.

Good luck and happy writing. Contact me at www. scriptadvice.co.uk to put into practice what this book outlines.

USEFUL RESOURCES

https://scriptpdf.com/
Free to download Academy Award Winning Features, TV scripts from greats like Shonda Rhimes, resources and scripting tools and featured scripts.

https://www.bbc.com/mediacentre/bbcstudios/2022/bbc-studios-writers-academy-2022-new-focus-original-development
Information on how to apply for Script Works workshops and training plus development initiatives and lectures from visiting tv writer alumni, all part of the training and development offered by the Writers' Academy out of BBC Studios.

https://www.bbc.co.uk/writersroom/
Opportunities and tips and tricks for new and experienced writers of television. Useful BBC Library where transmitted scripts can be downloaded.

https://scriptmag.com/features/tv-writing-tips-and-tricks-how-to-write-a-series-drama

Script is a useful resource for writers of tv and features. Great articles on writing and tips and tricks from me and other experienced writers/producers/consultants both in the UK and the USA.

https://www.inktip.com/article_single.php?a_id=180
Inktip is another great screenwriting resource magazine for tv and feature writers. I contributed some useful articles to this USA popular magazine.

https://www.screenskills.com/
This training and development initiative is useful for those wanting to learn a new skill or enhance their current skill base in the areas of development, writing and production. My popular course Script Editing for Television was initially funded by this organisation and currently bursaries for fees, travel and accommodation are regularly granted for attendees to my course.

RECOMMENDED
SCRIPT COMPETITIONS

https://bluecatscreenplay.com/
Good resource website run by Gordy Seymour Hoffman.
I think this outfit genuinely cares for writers and the
promotion of their voices to the industry. Their competition
is respected in the industry and you will have good feedback
in any event, from experienced readers in the USA.

https://www.bafta.org/supporting-talent/rocliffe
I rate this initiative which is consistently putting new writers
and the development of their voices first. Their script
competition is a genuine way to get your work out there,
read, analysed and if placed, this will help advance your
writing career for the UK and beyond.

https://redplanetpictures.co.uk/the-red-planet-prize
Worth keeping this one bookmarked. Red Planet have run
a highly reputable script competition for several years now
and genuinely give a leg up to new writers and their projects
via this competition.

https://www.intercompetition.com/archive/writing/ad/sir-peter-ustinov-television-scriptwriting-award,2648

This tv script competition is hugely respected in the industry, however the submission criteria has an age range limit to new writers up to the age of 30 years only.

ACKNOWLEDGEMENTS

I am very fortunate to be able to say that as a script editor starting out, I was able to work with writers who were then on a strong trajectory to tv domination and have now smashed through that ceiling and are rightly at the top of their game. These writers inspired me to do a better a job, to dig in to why they wrote like they did and to help them deliver their stories to the small screen. I was carried along by their passion, for the craft of television writing and by the whole exciting process of making up stories for a living. My enthusiasm for this work has never diminished. Thank you Tony McHale, Tony Jordan, Ashley Pharoah, Sally Wainwright, Peter Whalley, Patrea Smallacombe, Paul Abbot, Kay Mellor and Russell T Davies.

If you enjoyed *From Creation to Pitch*, look out *Writing for Television* by Yvonne Grace

'A very comprehensive and informative book on TV script writing. Yvonne covers every conceivable point that will help writers wanting to break into writing for the small screen, whilst at the same time creating a very accessible read'
SANCTUARY FILMS

'Offers valuable insight, sage advice and a wealth of information'
DOMINIC CARVER

A no-nonsense, direct down-the-lens look at the television industry written from the point of view of a television drama producer who's been there, done it, fought some battles and won the odd award.

Written in an engaging, anecdotal tone, *Writing for Television* provides advice on:

- Getting an agent
- The type of writer television's looking for
- The tool kit a television writer needs
- The writer /script editor relationship
- How to structure a storyline
- How to write good treatments and outlines

Packed full of useful insights, links and information, the book includes interviews with successful television writers working today, pointers on how to work collaboratively in the industry and how to make good contacts with the people who can further your career.

KAMERABOOKS.CO.UK/WRITING-FOR-TELEVISION

**Looking to learn more from successful screenwriters?
Why not try *The Art of Screen Adaptation*
by Alistair Owen?**

'Fascinating'
SUNDAY TIMES

'A formidable repository of knowledge and experience,
and a great resource for fledgling screenwriters
and film fans alike'
ROGER MICHELL

Hollywood. Netflix. Amazon. BBC. Producers and audiences are hungrier than ever for stories, and a lot of those stories begin life as a book – but how exactly do you transfer a story from the page to the screen? Do adaptations use the same creative gears as original screenplays? Does a true story give a project more weight than a fictional one? Is it helpful to have the original author's input on the script? And how much pressure is the screenwriter under, knowing they won't be able to please everyone with the finished product?

Alistair Owen puts all these questions and many more to some of the top names in screenwriting, including Hossein Amini (*Drive*), Moira Buffini (*Jane Eyre*), Nick Hornby (*An Education*), Deborah Moggach (*Pride & Prejudice*) and David Nicholls (*Patrick Melrose*).

Exploring fiction and nonfiction projects, contemporary and classic books, films and TV series, *The Art of Screen Adaptation* reveals the challenges and pleasures of reimagining stories for cinema and television and provides a frank and fascinating masterclass with the writers who have done it – and have the awards and acclaim to show for it.

KAMERABOOKS.CO.UK/THE-ART-OF-SCREEN-ADAPTATION

●LDCASTLE BOOKS

POSSIBLY THE UK'S SMALLEST
INDEPENDENT PUBLISHING GROUP

Oldcastle Books is an independent publishing company formed in 1985 dedicated to providing an eclectic range of titles with a nod to the popular culture of the day.

Imprints vary from the award winning crime fiction list, NO EXIT PRESS (now part of Bedford Square Publishers), to lists about the film industry, KAMERA BOOKS & CREATIVE ESSENTIALS. We have dabbled in the classics, with PULP! THE CLASSICS, taken a punt on gambling books with HIGH STAKES, provided in-depth overviews with POCKET ESSENTIALS and covered a wide range in the eponymous OLDCASTLE BOOKS list. Most recently we have welcomed two new sister imprints with THE CRIME & MYSTERY CLUB and VERVE, home to great, original, page-turning fiction.

oldcastlebooks.com

   kamera BOOKS creative ESSENTIALS HIGH STAKES

| OLDCASTLE BOOKS | KAMERA BOOKS | HIGHSTAKES PUBLISHING
| POCKET ESSENTIALS | CREATIVE ESSENTIALS | THE CRIME & MYSTERY CLUB
| NO EXIT PRESS | PULP! THE CLASSICS | VERVE BOOKS